ABERDEEN UNIVERSITY STUDIES
General Editor:
JOHN MACKINTOSH, M.A.
NUMBER 147

PAPERS
MAINLY SHAKESPEARIAN

PAPERS
MAINLY
SHAKESPEARIAN

COLLECTED BY

G. I. DUTHIE

Published for the University of Aberdeen
OLIVER AND BOYD
EDINBURGH: TWEEDDALE COURT
LONDON: 39A WELBECK STREET, W.I.

FIRST PUBLISHED .   .   . 1964

PRINTED IN GREAT BRITAIN AT THE UNIVERSITY PRESS, ABERDEEN
FOR OLIVER AND BOYD LTD., EDINBURGH

FOREWORD

The publication of this book has been sponsored by the University of Aberdeen, to mark the Shakespeare quatercentenary. All of the contributors have some connection with this University. Professor Sutherland and Mr. Jamieson are Aberdeen graduates: Professor Lawrenson is a former member of the staff; and Professor Gordon is a former external examiner. The remaining four authors are present members of the staff.

Thanks are due to the University Court and the University Studies Committee: to my fellow-contributors, whose co-operation has lightened my editorial task: to the publishers: and, especially, to Mr. John Mackintosh, the General Editor of the University Studies, who has given devoted and unsparing help at all stages in the preparation of the volume for publication.

G. I. D.

King's College
Aberdeen

CONTENTS

John M. Lothian

ADAM SMITH AS A CRITIC OF SHAKESPEARE

The discovery of a student's verbatim notes [1] of his Lectures on Rhetoric and Belles Lettres adds greatly to our knowledge of both Adam Smith's character and tastes and of his views on Literature. Prior to the discovery it had been known from his own essays contributed to the abortive *Edinburgh Review* of 1755, from snatches in Boswell, and from the contributions (to Anderson's *The Bee* in 1791) of one who had interviewed him, that his bias lay towards French classicism in poetry and drama. He preferred rhyme to blank verse, order and propriety to careless energy, and, in general, he thought that writers (and readers) should comport themselves like gentlemen.

From a reading of the new Lectures, Smith emerges as a considerable critic. We are not concerned here with his lengthy discussion of the principles of good composition, especially in narration and in description, though in a sense they are all relevant to the later comments that he makes on particular authors. He applies his principles in some detail to Addison and Swift, Temple and Shaftesbury, and comments very fully on the classical orators and historians.

Smith's first significant mention of Shakespeare comes in his discussion of metaphor. Two metaphors, he thinks, should "never be run together, as in that case they can never both be just". Shakespeare, he finds,[2] "is often guilty of this fault, as in the line immediately following that before cited, when he goes on '*or bravely arm ourselves and stem a sea of troubles*'. [Smith, like Hazlitt, has an excellent but inexact memory!] Here there is plain absurdity, as there is no meaning in one's putting on armour to stem the sea." "Shakespeare's 'sea of troubles' ", he adds, "has been converted in a late edition into a 'siedge', but the former reading is so like Shakespeare's manner that I dare to say he wrote it so." He goes on to illustrate a similar confusion in the first few lines of Thomson's *Spring*.

On the other hand, Smith had found something to commend in the image used by Shakespeare in the line preceding the "sea of troubles". "When the alteration of the word is in its signification, it must either be in giving it one to which it has some resemblance or analogy, or when it gets one to which it has no resemblance but is in some way connected. Thus when we say *the slings and arrows of adverse [sic] fortune*, there is some connection betwixt the crosses of bad fortune and the slings and arrows of an enemy."[3] Later, in briefly describing metonymy and allegory, he adds, "Had Spenser been able to use that comparison (of the arrows of bad fortune to the uneasiness of bad fortune) he would have described fortune in a certain garb, throwing her darts around her, and wounding those that were under her power".[4]

When he comes to discuss the art of description in narration Smith distinguishes two ways of conveying the idea "of a fact that is grand, either by describing it and enumerating various particulars that concern it, or by relating the effect that it has on those who behold it".[5] The first he would call the direct method, the other the indirect. Milton, he finds, uses the first in his description of Paradise, and in Satan's view of the burning lake, the second in Adam's account of the effect of Eve's presence on him. Shakespeare uses the indirect method in *King Lear*, in the description of Dover Cliff. This method, he later considers, "is in most cases by far the best. We see accordingly Shakespeare's descriptions are greatly more animated than those of Spenser. Shakespeare, as he wrote in dialogues, had it always in his power to make the persons of the dialogue relate the effects any object had upon them. Spenser describes everything directly, and has in adhering to this plan described several objects directly which no other author attempted in that manner. [Spenser was constrained to take this method because he dealt in allegorical personages, without existence or form but what he conferred on them.]"[6] He goes on to show that Pindar, Homer, and Milton never describe music directly, and that Shakespeare, in the *Merchant of Venice*, describes it by the effect it produces. "But this", he adds, i.e. describing music directly, "which none of these great men ever attempted, Spenser has not only attempted, but has succeeded in, in the account of the Knight of Temperance destroying the Bower of Bliss."[7]

In his fourteenth Lecture, Smith both enlarges on and lists seriatim the points of his advice on the art of describing objects "either corporeal or non-corporeal", "natural or artificial", existing "completely at the same time" or "subsisting in a succession of incidents". With the eighth piece of advice he ends: "It would appear needless to guard you against using epithets that are contradictory or not applicable to the object, if we did not find that some of the greatest English writers have fallen into it, in many places. Mr. Pope frequently applies adjectives to substantives with which they cannot at all agree, as when he speaks of the *brown horror of the groves*. 'Brown' joined to 'horror' conveys no idea at all. Thomson is often guilty of this fault, and Shakespeare almost continually."[8]

These incidental references to Shakespeare and almost casual use of illustrations from his works hardly exhibit the strong analytical powers of Smith as a critic of literature. One would have to follow him through the long courses of critical analysis (which he frequently uses) of the various methods, devices, and effects to be adopted or devised in the literary art, to appreciate his powers to the full: and that is not called for here. But it is when he turns to the theatre, and the art and practice of the drama, that Smith shows himself—as he calls Dionysius of Halicarnassus—a "penetrating" critic, if not "too refined", as he thinks Dionysius to be. For Smith is very much at home in the drama. A close friend of his later years, Andrew Dalzel, the Professor of Greek at Edinburgh, recorded that he often found Smith perusing the classics, especially the dramatists of Greece and Rome, and declaring that "the best amusement of age was to renew acquaintance with the writers who were the delight of one's youth".[9] The only classical play he mentions by name in the Lectures is Aristophanes' *Clouds*. He refers to Euripides' prologues, and to Sophocles' observing of the unity of place. But it is obvious that his taste has been formed upon them, and that he is deeply versed in their chief critic and expositor, Aristotle. He moves easily among the dramatists of his own and of the previous age—Young, (whose *Revenge* he dubs "*Othello* spoiled"), Otway, Dryden, Lee, Addison, Racine, Corneille, and the "Italian Comedians at Paris".

In tragedy, Smith finds, it is not the newness—"the only merit of a novel"—that keeps us interested, but "the importance of the narration". Virgil and Homer both inform us in the beginning of the chief events that are told in the whole poem. "Even in tragedy, where it is reckoned an essential part to keep the plot in suspense, this is not so necessary as in romance. A tragedy can bear to be read again and again. Though the incidents are not new to us, they are new to the actors, and by this means interest us, as well as by their own importance. (The gradual and just development of the catastrophe constitutes a great beauty in every tragedy, yet it is not a necessary one, otherwise we could never with any pleasure hear or see acted a play for the second time: yet that pleasure often grows by repetition.)" He goes on to show that Euripides, by means of a god or a ghost in his Prologues, acquaints us beforehand with what is to happen, "that we may be free to attend to the sentiment and the action of each scene, some of which he has laboured greatly".[10]

Though Smith realizes that tragedy for the most part deals with "an old tale", so that novelty is not important, he is yet prepared to allow the tragic writer—and others, for that matter,—to make what alterations they will, for it is entertainment that we are looking for. "As we know that no story is so completely ridiculous as to tell well without some cobbling, so we know that no series of adventures are so entirely of a piece, either so wonderful and extraordinary, or so lamentable, or so absurd, that they could completely answer the design of a poet without some improvement. We therefore allow the tragic writer whose subject is the lamentable, the comic writer who has pitched on the ridiculous and absurd for his subject, and the epic poet who endeavours to interest us by a series of grand and extraordinary events, each to model his story (or even sometimes to invent one) so as to make it all suitable to this end."[11]

Smith would thus allow dramatists, including Shakespeare, a free hand in altering well-known stories, even historical facts, for their purpose, since the design of all is to entertain. There is, however, one requisite in his opinion "absolutely necessary both to epic and dramatic writing, that is, unity of interest". Though "the greatest of critics" have laboured to show in what it is that this requisite consists, "it is no more than this: that every part of the story should tend to some one end, whatever that be. . . . In the same manner as a story-teller would appear to have failed in his design of raising our laughter . . . if he should bring in anything of a grave and serious nature, so it is necessary that the poet should accommodate all his circumstances so as that they tend to bring about the main event either directly or indirectly. A comic writer should make all the parts tend to excite our sense of ridicule, and at least conclude the work with the highest piece of ridicule, which all the rest pointed at or tended some way to bring about. The tragic writer must in the same manner make all the parts of the action of a lamentable nature, or some way tend to bring about the great catastrophe; and so of the epic writer."[12]

Smith is violently opposed to any "mixture" of the kinds. "Tragi-comedy", he says, "though the different parts be very well executed, and may be very interesting, is yet a monstrous production." In Dryden's *Spanish Friar*, for instance, "the tragical part is very good, and the comic part is admirable, so that the whole is no bad piece; but the parts had been much better taken separate; the effect of the one would not have contra-dicted the other". Equally he objects to the scene of the grave-diggers in *Hamlet*. "Though a very good scene in its sort, it had better been away, as it has no share in bringing about the main design of the piece, and is some-what contrary to the temper of the rest of the scenes."[13]

Smith finds that the unity in tragedy differs from that of comedy because of the different relative importance of character and plot in each. "In comic writings", he observes, "the ridicule must consist in the characters represented: ridicule that is founded only on the ridiculousness of the circumstances into which the persons are brought, without regarding themselves, is the lowest species of wit, and such as is hardly tolerable in a common story. On the other hand, in tragedy or epic poetry the chief art does not consist in displaying the characters, but in showing in what manner the chief persons in whom we are chiefly concerned acted in lamentable or difficult circumstances, and how at last they were either, in the first, altogether oppressed by their misfortunes or extricated themselves from them." He concludes, therefore, that "the unity in comedy consists in the characters; whereas in tragedy or epic poetry it consists chiefly in managing the circumstances. But in no part should anything appear to have a contrary tendency to that of the whole piece."[14]

What Smith calls the "unity of interest" must, I think, be equated with what Johnson called "the unity of action". Shakespeare, Johnson found, "has not . . . an intrigue regularly perplexed and regularly unravelled. . . . But his plan has commonly what Aristotle requires, a beginning, a middle, and an end; one event is concatenated with another and the conclusion follows by easy consequence."[15] Smith, like Johnson and Aristotle before him, found the core of a play to lie in the *nexus* of events, the warp of character in the woof of circumstance, not in the presentation of character or of a state of mind.

When he comes to discuss the Unities of Time and of Place, Smith in these lectures of 1762-63, which indeed may date from many years earlier, in some ways anticipates curiously the views of Johnson expressed in his *Preface to Shakespeare* (1765). The pair were of too positive a nature, too given to pontificate in company, ever to get on well together, and legend has it that when the two first met, Johnson's report at a later date to Boswell, "Sir, I was once in company with Smith, and we did not take to each other", was a very much watered-down version of the battle of vituperatives that took place. But on the question of what the spectator of a play actually feels, the positive—and limited—nature of the two men, as with the question of the relative merits of rhyme and blank verse, brings them together. "The truth is", says Johnson, "that the spectators are always in their senses, and know from the first act to the last, that the stage is only a stage, and that the players are only players."[16]

Smith arrives at the same basic position, but by a different route, and the inferences he draws are very different. He contrasts the tasks of the writers of epic and of drama, in presenting the same story. "As the one is carried on by dialogue, the connection betwixt two parts can only be kept up by the changing of the persons; whereas in the other the poet can, in a few words, in his own person, keep up the connection. The actions of a year would take up a year to represent them; but a poet can dispatch them in two or three words."[17]

From this analysis of the basic difference in the treatment of time, Smith passes to a discussion of the actual practice of the dramatists. "Shakespeare and some other English writers", he says, "have been chiefly guilty of omitting this; the French are generally very little. Racine never supposes more time to have been taken up in the actions than in the representations. Shakespeare, on the other hand, supposes often that three or four years have elapsed betwixt one scene and another." Such gaps are usually considered to have a bad effect on us, and the reason generally given for this is "that it prevents our deception. We cannot suppose that when we have been but half-an-hour in the playhouse that two or three years have passed. But in reality we are never thus deceived. We know that we are in the playhouse, that the persons before us are actors, and that the thing represented either happened before, or perhaps never happened at all. The pleasure we have in a dramatical performance no more rises from deception than that which we have in looking at pictures. No one ever imagined that he saw the sacrifice of Iphigenia; no more did anyone imagine that he saw King Richard the Third. Everyone knows that at the one time he saw a picture, and at the other Mr. Garrick, or some other actor."[18]

Smith is convinced that the bad effects of failure to observe the Unity of Time have another explanation than the "interruption of deception"; " 'tis rather from the uneasiness we fell in being kept in the dark with regard to what happened in so long a time. When, in the scene before us, there is supposed to have passed three or four years before the last was before us, we immediately become uneasy to know what has happened during that time. Many important events must have happened in that time of which we know nothing. We make a jump from one time to another, without knowing what connected them. The same jump is often made in epic poets; but then they take care to smooth it over by telling us in a few words what happened in that time. Was this small connection omitted, the jump would be as uneasy in the dramatic poem as the dramatical performance."[19] He then proceeds to illustrate the comparable ineffectiveness of historical and other pictures to portray a sequence of events. In both drama and painting, he claims, "it is not the preventing our deception" which makes us uneasy, as appears "from this, that we are not very uneasy at a small interruption: we can easily perceive what may have passed during the hour or so for which the action is suspended. We see also that these pieces, though they have not the effect they would have were it not for this defect, have yet a very considerable one, which would not be the case if the whole pleasure we take in dramatical works proceeded from the deception."[20]

The same principle—that it is not deception or illusion that gives us the pleasure in drama—is used by Smith to determine his attitude to breaches of the Unity of Place, and again it is his consuming interest in "what happens in the intervals" not presented on the stage that troubles the critic. Johnson dismisses the entire problem with a devastating sweep of his Gargantuan hand. "He that can take the stage at one time for the palace of the Ptolemies, may take it in half an hour for the promontory of Actium. Delusion, if delusion be admitted, has no certain limitations; if the spectator can be once persuaded that his old acquaintance are Alexander and Caesar, that a room illuminated with candles is the plain of Pharsalia, or the bank of Granicus, he is in a state of elevation above the reach of reason or of truth, and from the heights of empyrean poetry may despise the circumscriptions of terrestrial nature."[21]

Compared with this powerful declaration Smith's protests seem puny and pusillanimous. "In dramatic works", he declares, "the Unity of Place cannot be altogether maintained unless the action is such as that it be all supposed to be transacted in the same place, as well as at one time. Shakespeare in some of his plays breaks through this rule altogether: he makes one scene be in France, and the following one in England; one in London, and another at York, etc. In this case the distance is so great that we are anxious to know what has happened in the interval between them. The best way, surely, is to fix the action to one place if possible, as Racine and Sophocles have done; and if that is not possible, we should make the distance as little as possible, confining the action to the same house or thereabouts."[22] He adds, however, as in his discussion of the Unity of Time, that though the Unity of Place is not "observed, we find the effect of the piece may still be very considerable", which shows again, he thinks, that it is not deception that gives us pleasure in these works, and, in fact, "we are not deceived for one moment".[23] Smith's curiosity as to how the intervals of space or time in the action were to be filled leads him to object to any break in the continuity, even though there is no question of preserving "deception" or illusion; Johnson would brush the objection aside as quibbling: if we can imagine we are in one place or time, we can imagine we are in another soon after: actually we never delude ourselves in the theatre at all. His answer to Smith would in all probability have been, "Why bother about what happened in the intervals? If they had been important they should have been recorded."

While they are in general agreement on the Unities of Place and Time, though for different reasons, the two men are far from seeing eye to eye on Propriety of Character. Johnson is not convinced, as were Sidney and the Renaissance critics generally, that comedy should be confined to "low" characters, tragedy to "high". "Some", he says, "make comedy a representation of mean, and others of bad men. But any man's reflections will inform him, that every dramatic composition which raises mirth, is comic, and that, to raise mirth, it is by no means universally necessary, that the personages should be either mean or corrupt, nor always requisite, that the action should be trivial, nor ever, that it should be fictitious." Similarly, the presence of "great personages",—"monarchs and generals and guards" did not necessarily produce the awe of tragedy. "They have not considered that thoughts or incidents, in themselves ridiculous, grow still more grotesque by the solemnity of such characters . . . that what is despicable and abused, will not, by any association with splendid titles, become rational or great . . . and that the robes of royalty can give no dignity to nonsense or to folly."[24]

Smith comes upon us with an argument in support of the older viewpoint in the style of the "natural" historian of manners that does little credit to his estimate of human nature. "As comedy and tragedy", he maintains, "are designed to produce very different effects, so the characters they place as the principal ones must be such as are suited to produce these contrary effects. . . . Kings and nobles are what make the best characters in a tragedy. . . . We are too much accustomed to the misfortunes of people below or equal with ourselves to be greatly affected by them. But the misfortunes of the great, both as they seem connected with the welfare of a multitude, and as we are apt to pay great respect and attention to our superiors, however unworthy, are what chiefly affect us. Nay, such is the temper of men, that we are rather disposed to laugh at the misfortunes of our inferiors than take part in them. . . . 'Tis for this same principle that persons of high rank make very bad actors in a comedy. Dukes and princes and men of high rank, though they be never so ridiculous in themselves, never appear the subject of laughter. The same prejudice which makes us be so highly interested in their misfortunes, makes us also imagine there is something respectable even in their follies. Persons of low life, either equal or inferior to ourselves, are the best characters for comedy. We can laugh heartily at the absurdity of a shoe-maker or a burgess, though we can hardly prevail on ourselves to weep at his misfortunes. Farces, where the characters are the lowest of any, make us laugh more than the finest comedy; and on the other hand, we can hardly enter into the humour of a comedy of the highest sort, where dukes and nobles are the objects of our laughter. . . . We even carry this so far that we are rather apt to make sport of the misfortunes of our inferiors, than sympathize with them."[25] Johnson, to be sure, was no "leveller", but his views on the inherently comic character of many human situations, irrespective of the rank of those participating, were certainly on a firmer foundation of normal experience than those of the very class-conscious, mob-despising economist.

Since, for Smith, "the ridiculousness of comedy consists in the ridiculousness of the characters, and not of the circumstances", it is necessary that these should be a greater variety of characters in comedy than in tragedy. "We cannot always be laughing at misers or fops; we must have a variety of characters, to make the pieces agreeable."[26] In tragedy or in epic poetry, since "the adventures or circumstances, and the behaviour of the different persons in these circumstances, is what chiefly interest us", such variety of characters is not called for. Neither in Virgil nor Racine is there variety of character; there is no variety in the *Aeneid* at all. Racine's "men are all of one sort, and his women also have all the same character". When we consider that these authors are among the very best of their kind, "and yet have not the smallest share in this beauty " [*sc.* variety of character], "we will be apt to think it is not so very essential".[27] He thinks it likely that Virgil and Racine found it impossible to pay as much attention to propriety, decorum, and uniformity as they did and yet bring in a variety of characters. He finds them in this respect greatly inferior to Homer and Shakespeare. "The first of these has a vast variety of characters, and the latter still greater. But then this vast variety has often led them into breaches of decency, propriety, and uniformity of interest. As Racine seems to have studied these last-mentioned perfections still more than Virgil, so he has still less variety of character. And in the same manner Shakespeare, as the inconceivable variety of characters he has introduced far exceeds that of Homer's, so he has paid still less regard to decency and propriety." He concludes by holding the balance evenly between the contrasted virtues. "These different beauties of decorum and variety seem incompatible when in their greatest perfection, and we are not to condemn one who excels in the one as not being equally excellent in the other."[28]

While he is interested in the propriety of the characters as Shakespeare creates them in particular circumstances, and in their enormous variety, Smith surprisingly is not much interested in the characters for themselves. Yet, as the Lectures very fully show, he was fascinated by the work of Theophrastus and of La Bruyère, and analysed their methods at considerable length; he had studied the art of the historian Tacitus in character-drawing, and himself attempts sketches of the characters of Swift and of

Temple, as exemplifying the "plain" man and the "simple" man respectively: but of the sort of analysis that was soon to be exhibited in Morgann's essay on Falstaff or Richardson's studies of Richard III, Lear, Timon, and Hamlet, Smith has nothing.

NOTES

1. Adam Smith: *Lectures on Rhetoric and Belles Lettres 1762-63*, edited by John M. Lothian, 1963. References throughout this paper will be to Smith, *Rhetoric*.
2. Smith, *Rhetoric*, p. 27.
3. *Ibid*. p. 25.
4. *Ibid*. p. 27.
5. *Ibid*. p. 60.
6. *Ibid*. p. 63.
7. *Ibid*. p. 63.
8. *Ibid*. p. 73.
9. J. Rae, *Life of Adam Smith* (London, 1895), p. 23.
10. Smith, *Rhetoric*, p. 92.
11. *Ibid*. p. 116.
12. *Ibid*. p. 116-17.
13. *Ibid*. p. 117.
14. *Ibid*. p. 117.
15. S. Johnson: *Johnson on Shakespeare*, ed. Raleigh (1908), p. 25.
16. *Ibid*. p. 27.
17. Smith, *Rhetoric*, p. 118.
18. *Ibid*. p. 118.
19. *Ibid*. p. 118.
20. *Ibid*. p. 119.
21. Raleigh: *Johnson on Shakespeare*, p. 26.
22. Smith, *Rhetoric*, p. 119.
23. *Ibid*. p. 119.
24. *Rambler*, No. 125.
25. Smith, *Rhetoric*, p. 120.
26. *Ibid*. p. 121.
27. *Ibid*. p. 121.
28. *Ibid*. p. 122.

James Sutherland

THE MOVING PATTERN
OF SHAKESPEARE'S THOUGHT

One of the advantages which Shakespeare had over almost all his dramatic contemporaries lay in his ability to shape long speeches, passages, and even whole scenes in a continuously developing movement. At the risk of mixing my metaphors I propose to refer to this process as a moving pattern; for although it is the movement itself that immediately attracts and holds our attention, it is our awareness of the way in which that movement is controlled and organized and ultimately completed that gives to such speeches and passages their memorable quality.

This shaping power was present in Shakespeare from the first, but in the earliest plays it often expressed itself in a kind of pattern which I do not intend to discuss. What we often have in the early histories and comedies is much elaborately balanced writing, but this is for the most part static, deliberate, and artificial. It will be found in the long and beautiful speech of Henry VI (*3 Henry VI*, II. v.) when he has retired from the battlefield to muse upon the happy life of a homely swain in contrast with the life of anxieties which is the lot of a king. It will be found again, on many occasions, in *Richard III*; e.g. in the passage beginning, "I had an Edward, till a Richard kill'd him" (IV. iv. 40 ff.), where Queen Margaret and the Duchess of York chant alternate laments; or again, at II. ii. 74 ff. ("What stay had I but Edward? and he's gone"), where Queen Elizabeth, the two children of the murdered Clarence, and the Duchess's utter grief-stricken ejaculations, which are again characterized by repetition with variation. Formally balanced speeches, often with all the beauty of Elizabethan lyric, occur frequently in the early comedies, as in Valentine's soliloquy in *The Two Gentlemen of Verona*, III. i. 174 ff.:

> What light is light, if Silvia be not seen?
> What joy is joy, if Silvia be not by?
> Unless it be to think that she is by
> And feed upon the shadow of perfection.
> Except I be by Silvia in the night,
> There is no music in the nightingale;
> Unless I look on Silvia in the day,
> There is no day for me to look upon. . . .[1]

However lovely it may be, such a passage holds up the action of the play while Valentine allows himself to "tune a deploring dump", and although his poetical statement may be said to advance to some sort of climax, its component parts could be arranged in a different sequence without seriously disturbing the argument.

Yet even in the earliest plays there occur some passages which appear to generate energy from their own forward movement, and which at the same time store that energy because the formal development of the passage contains and concentrates it. When we come upon such passages they are often to be associated with the fact that one of Shakespeare's characters is putting a case, advocating some line of action, exercising his powers of persuasion in one way or another. For a supreme example of this type of speech we could turn to the famous oration pronounced by Antony over the dead body of Caesar; but much earlier than *Julius Caesar* we can see how ready Shakespeare is to avail himself of any natural opening for a display of forensic eloquence (a fact no doubt noted by the Baconians), and how such opportunities give added life to his writing. That he could, at so early a stage in his dramatic career, do this sort of thing so well may be in part accounted for by the education in rhetoric that he, in common with other Elizabethan boys, had received at school, and to the keen interest in rhetoric that is so marked a feature of the age. For an example of his ability to put a case, I turn to a passage in what is probably his first play, a speech of Queen Margaret in *2 Henry VI* (III. i. 4 ff.). The Queen, along with most of the nobles, is plotting the downfall of Humphrey, Duke of Gloucester, the King's uncle. The Duke has been summoned to a parliament at St. Edmondsbury, but when the scene opens he has not yet arrived.

> *King.*   I muse my Lord of Gloucester is not come:
> 'Tis not his wont to be the hindmost man,
> Whate'er occasion keeps him from us now.
>
> *Queen.*   Can you not see? or will ye not observe
> The strangeness of his alter'd countenance?
> With what a majesty he bears himself,
> How insolent of late he is become,
> How proud, how peremptory, and unlike himself?
> We know the time since he was mild and affable,
> And if we did but glance a far-off look,
> Immediately he was upon his knee,
> That all the court admired him for submission:
> But meet him now, and, be it in the morn,
> When every one will give the time of day,
> He knits his brow and shows an angry eye
> And passeth by with stiff unbowed knee,
> Disdaining duty that to us belongs.
> Small curs are not regarded when they grin
> But great men tremble when the lion roars;
> And Humphrey is no little man in England.
> First note that he is near you in descent,
> And should you fall, he is the next will mount.
> Me seemeth then it is no policy,
> Respecting what a rancorous mind he bears
> And his advantage following your decease,
> That he should come about your royal person

Or be admitted to your highness' council.
By flattery hath he won the commons' hearts,
And when he please to make commotion,
'Tis to be fear'd they all will follow him.
Now 'tis the spring, and weeds are shallow-rooted;
Suffer them now, and they'll o'ergrow the garden
And choke the herbs for want of husbandry.
The reverent care I bear unto my lord
Made me collect these dangers in the duke.
If it be fond, call it a woman's fear;
Which fear if better reasons can supplant,
I will subscribe, and say I wrong'd the duke. . . .

Here already we have a well-organized argument; the speech of the Queen is an apparently reasonable and well-founded complaint, but is in fact a subtle appeal to prejudice. The mind of the King has to be turned against the one honest man in his court (for so he is represented in Shakespeare's play), and the Queen opens her case with the skill of an accomplished pleader. First of all we have the appeal, always an effective one, to the King's own observation: a series of reiterated questions, rising to a climax as the supposed evidence builds up to an apparently unanswerable proof. The Queen is on sure ground here: none of us likes to think that other people have observed what we have failed to notice for ourselves. Henry is already shaken. The Queen now shifts her ground, and the questions give place to a series of statements as she contrasts Gloucester's present behaviour with his more obsequious conduct a little while ago. This contrast would be effective merely *as* contrast between past (given to us in the form of direct statement) and present (suggested to us in the form of damaging questions), but it is doubly effective because her statements seem to lend support to the allegations that she has just made; for the Queen, in appealing to Henry's recollections of the past behaviour of his uncle, which he knows to have been always dutiful and respectful (as she has just said), seems to be establishing her case for his present behaviour being of quite a different kind. If one half of her statement is true, why should not the other half be true too? No doubt if Gloucester were to appear at this point his behaviour towards the King would immediately disprove the Queen's allegation, but he is not yet there to justify himself; the Queen's case against him therefore rests upon a confusing appeal to the King's visual memory which at this moment he is unable to check.

Having now succeeded in planting suspicion in the mind of her husband, the Queen passes on to a statement of general validity—

Small curs are not regarded when they grin;
But great men tremble when the lion roars—

which, since exception cannot be taken to it, seems again to confirm the validity of the charges she is making, and which she immediately presses home to the point at issue—

And Humphrey is no little man in England!

What follows is a series of reasons why the King should be especially wary
of this powerful nobleman: he is next in succession to the throne, and his
rancorous and ambitious mind (already demonstrated!) is bound to make
him a dangerous rival—all the more so since he is popular with the people
and would have little difficulty in stirring them up to rebellion. The
Queen's arguments here are again a clever mixture of truth and falsehood,
but there is enough truth in them—Gloucester *is* next in succession, he *is*
popular with the people—to make her baseless charges seem at least
plausible. Still, the King has hitherto had every reason to trust Gloucester,
and has been accustomed to lean upon him for support: the Queen cannot
therefore risk shocking him into protest by openly calling for the liquida-
tion of the powerful duke, and so she says what she means without
actually saying it:

> Now 'tis the spring, and weeds are shallow-rooted;
> Suffer them now, and they'll o'ergrow the garden. . . .

The metaphors serve to wrap up the nakedness of the Queen's meaning,
and the *general* truth of the statement ("if you don't get rid of weeds while
they are still young they will end by choking your plants") takes off some
of the immediacy of its application to Gloucester. The Queen has now
concluded her case, and her speech ends on a quiet and reasonable note,
with a tactful expression of solicitude for the King's welfare, an admission
of her natural fears as a woman, and a modest willingness to admit that she
may be wrong if more experienced heads than hers should not agree with
her interpretation of the facts.

I do not wish to make extravagant claims for this speech, but dramatically it is well above the normal level of the play, which is in general rather
flat and monotonous. It does not hold our interest by means of its metaphors, which are neither numerous nor in themselves remarkable, but by
the colloquial liveliness of the expression (e.g. "And Humphrey is no
little man in England") and the skill with which the argument is carried
forward. The pressure of that argument on the minds of the King and of
the audience is maintained by the Queen's insistent plucking on one
string, and yet, as the argument develops, there are many changes of
pace and emphasis, changes of direction, and much variety of pitch. How
genuinely colloquial the Queen's speech is may be seen from an examination of the first few lines. I am indebted to my colleague, Professor
Randolph Quirk, for providing me with what is called a prosodic transcription of this passage, after I had spoken it into a tape-recorder.

The prosodic transcription is by my colleague Mr. Derek Davy, of the
Survey of English Usage, University College, London. The conventions
may be summarized as follows:

(#) . . . #   end of tone-unit or (if prefixed) prosodic modification
/   first point of pitch prominence in tone-unit
[   ]   subordinate tone-unit

2*

JAMES SUTHERLAND

´ ∧ ∨ `	rising, rising-falling, falling-rising, and falling pitch contours respectively
·	before a syllable denotes continuation of pitch contour
; , : !	degrees of pitch height (from low to high at the beginning of a contour)
' ''	degrees of syllabic emphasis greater than normal
·	above a syllable-centre: clipped
a . . . a⧻	"allegro": a piece spoken at a tempo faster than normal
m . . . m⧻	"modulation": a piece spoken with the modulation marginally indicated

m: high, low: pitch height

m: glissando´: with rhythmic pulsation accompanied by pitch
       moving up from arsis to thesis

m: monotonous: pitch range

. - - - denote relative duration of pause,—corresponding to a foot

These conventions are further explained and discussed in "Studies in the Correspondence of Prosodic to Grammatical Features in English" by R. Quirk and others (*Proceedings of the Ninth International Congress of Linguists*, The Hague, 1964, pp. 483 ff.) and in *Systems of Paralanguage* by D. Crystal and R. Quirk (The Hague, 1964). In addition, a diæresis is used to show the trisyllabic form of "unbowëd".

	/Can you not ,sée⧻ . /or !will ye not ob,sérve⧻ the /[strángeness] [of his ,álter'd] ;cóuntenance⧻-
m: high	*m*/with what a ,''májesty he ·bears [him/sélf⧻]⧻ *m*⧻- how ''/ínsolent [of /láte⧻]⧻ . he /is becóme⧻ .
m: low	*m* /how próud⧻ /how péremptory⧻ . and un*m*⧻ ''/líke him·self⧻- -
	/wè know the time sínce⧻ he was /mild and !àffable⧻-
m: gliss´.	*a* and if we /did *a*⧻ but glânce⧻ a *m* /far-off lóok⧻ *m*⧻ .
m: monot.	im/mediately *m* he was upon his *m*⧻ knée⧻ . that /all the :court ad:mired him for submìssion⧻- - but /meet him :nôẇ⧻- and /be it in the mórn⧻
m: monot.	*m* when /every 'one will 'give the 'time of *m*⧻ dáy⧻- /he knits his brôw⧻ and /shows an ângry [/èye⧻]⧻- and /passeth !bỳ⧻ with /stiff un'bowëd :knèe⧻- dis/[daìning] :dùty⧻ that to /us be:lòngs⧻- - /smàll ·curs⧻ are /not re'garded when they ,grín⧻- but /great 'men !trèmble⧻ . /when the !lìon ,róars⧻- and ''/Hùmphrey⧻ /is no lîttle [/màn⧻] [in /Èngland⧻]⧻

Shakespeare never lost his interest in putting a case. Much of *Troilus and Cressida* is concerned with debates on policy, and Ulysses' famous speech "Time hath, my lord, a wallet at his back" (III. iii. 145 ff.) is another masterpiece of shapely and persuasive argument. The noble speech of Othello in Act I, scene i, where he answers Brabantio's charge that he has used witchcraft to obtain the love of Desdemona, is often thought of as a fine example of dramatic narrative, and so it is; but it is also Othello's justification of his actions, the plea he enters in his own defence, and it is shaped as it is owing to that fact. So, too, with the long speech of Hotspur in *1 Henry IV* (I. iii. 29 ff.), when he is taxed by the King with having failed to deliver his prisoners. Hotspur's reply to the King ("My liege, I did deny no prisoners") is one of the liveliest pieces of narrative that Shakespeare ever wrote, but again it is more than just that: it is, in Hotspur's rough and irrepressible eloquence, his answer to the charge that he is keeping those captured Scots "to his own use". As such, it is a picturesque and plausible statement of a case, but the impression of spontaneous feeling that it leaves on the mind of a reader or listener is largely due to the fact that it is also an expression of Hotspur's character and inflammable temper. What he really thought of the King's demand emerges clearly a little later (212 ff.) when the Earl of Worcester tries to make him see reason:

> *Wor.*   Those same noble Scots
> That are your prisoners—
> *Hot.*   I'll keep them all;
> By God, he shall not have a Scot of them;
> No, if a Scot would save his soul, he shall not. . . .

It is this angry feeling, more or less pent up in his long reply to the King but rumbling dangerously just beneath the surface, that gives to his speech its variety of pace and rhythm, and that is ultimately responsible for the form it takes.

Those two elements of character and strong feeling are clearly the shaping forces in many of Shakespeare's most memorable speeches. The effect of the dramatist's clear and powerful realization of an individual character on the mode in which that character will express himself hardly requires demonstration, but it is worth remarking that the first outstanding character in Shakespeare's drama is Richard III, and that, as Richard, Duke of Gloucester, in *3 Henry VI*, his speech is already individualized. In his long self-analysis in Act III, scene ii of that play he holds a kind of debate with himself, and his speech has the easy and natural movement of a man thinking on his feet. "In Shakespeare", Coleridge once remarked, "one sentence begets the next naturally; the meaning is all inwoven. He goes on kindling like a meteor through the dark atmosphere. . . ." [2] About a year later Coleridge returned to the same point, but made it with a different metaphor:

> Shakespeare's intellectual action is wholly unlike that of Ben Jonson, or Beaumont and Fletcher. The latter see the totality of a sentence or passage, and then project it entire. Shakespeare goes on creating and evolving *B* out of *A*, and *C* out of *B*, and so on, just as a serpent moves, which makes a fulcrum of its own body, and seems for ever twisting and untwisting its own strength. [3]

The speech of Richard just mentioned has all the marks of this creative process, working at a comparatively easy pressure:

> I'll make my heaven to dream upon *the crown*,
> And, whiles I live, to account this world but hell,
> Until my mis-shaped trunk that bears this head
> Be round impaled with a glorious *crown*.
> And yet I know not how to get *the crown*,
> For many lives stand between me and home:
> And I,—like one lost in a thorny wood,
> That *rends the thorns* and is *rent with the thorns*,
> *Seeking a way* and *straying from the way*;
> Not knowing how *to find* the open air,
> But toiling desperately *to find it out*,—
> *Torment* myself to catch the English crown:
> And from *that torment* I will free myself,
> Or hew my way out with a bloody axe. . . .

Far more striking examples of this "inwoven" meaning may be found in the later plays, but the process itself emerges clearly enough in Richard's musings.

For the effect of strong feeling on this moving pattern of thought I turn to a passage in *Richard III* (II. i. 103 ff.). King Edward has given an order for his brother Clarence to be put to death, but has then revoked it: Richard, however, has seen to it that the stay of execution never reaches the Lieutenant of the Tower, and Clarence is murdered by two of Richard's hired killers. The King is still stupefied by the news of his brother's death when the Earl of Derby comes rushing into the royal presence, and begs a pardon for one of his servants who has killed a retainer of the Duke of Norfolk. There is no specific source in Holinshed for the Earl of Derby's tactless intervention, but the proximate source is clearly to be found in the chronicler's account of Edward IV's remorse for the death of Clarence:

> Although king Edward were consenting to his death, yet he much did both lament his infortunate chance, & repent his sudden execution: insomuch that, when anie person sued to him for the pardon of malefactors condemned to death, he would accustomablie saie, & openlie speake: "Oh infortunate brother, for whose life not one would make sute!" [4]

It was clearly the King's words as recorded by Holinshed that suggested to Shakespeare the pattern of his passionate reply; and once started on the speech, he was carried forward on a wave of feeling by that process of empathy which enabled him, time after time, to *be* the character for whose thought and feeling he was finding the appropriate words.

> *King.* Have I a tongue to doom my brother's death,
> And shall the same give pardon to a slave?
> My brother slew no man; his fault was thought,
> And yet his punishment was cruel death.
> Who sued to me for him? who, in my rage,
> Kneel'd at my feet, and bade me be advised?
> Who spake of brotherhood? who spake of love?

Who told me how the poor soul did forsake
The mighty Warwick, and did fight for me?
Who told me, in the field by Tewkesbury,
When Oxford had me down, he rescued me,
And said, "Dear brother, live, and be a king"?
Who told me, when we both lay in the field
Frozen almost to death, how he did lap me
Even in his own garments, and gave himself,
All thin and naked, to the numb cold night?
All this from my remembrance brutish wrath
Sinfully pluck'd, and not a man of you
Had so much grace to put it in my mind.
But when your carters or your waiting-vassals
Have done a drunken slaughter, and defaced
The precious image of our dear Redeemer,
You straight are on your knees for pardon, pardon;
And I, unjustly too, must grant it you:
But for my brother, not a man would speak,
Nor I, ungracious, speak unto myself
For him, poor soul. The proudest of you all
Have been beholding to him in his life;
Yet none of you would once plead for his life.
O God, I fear thy justice will take hold
On me, and you, and mine, and yours for this!
Come, Hastings, help me to my closet. Oh, poor Clarence!

This is surely a perfect example of the moving pattern of Shakespeare's thought, psychologically and rhetorically irresistible. The short reiterated questions of the first seven lines give way to the more elaborate questions of the next nine lines, as the first movement reaches its climax. From those agitated questions the King's speech passes into its second movement, a series of equally emotional statements, "evolving B out of A, and C out of B". (There are some religious overtones, notably in the half-comparison of Clarence to the Good Samaritan, and in the overt reference to "the precious image of our dear Redeemer".) Under the controlling influence of his grief and indignation the King returns twice to an idea he has already expressed (. . . "not a man of you/Had so much grace to put it in my mind. . . . But for my brother, not a man would speak. . . . Yet none of you would once plead for his life."), and his indignation is shown again in the angry reiteration of "pardon, pardon". As for the way in which "one sentence begets the next naturally", we can see that at several points in the speech, but most obviously perhaps in the sequence of

> The proudest of you all
> Have been beholding to him *in his life*;
> Yet none of you would once plead *for his life* . . .

which, incidentally, brings the speech to its second main climax. The King's failing physical energy has now burnt itself out, and he ends, as so often in Shakespeare's impassioned speeches, on a "dying fall".

Shakespeare's ability to develop a patterned movement of thought in a way which seems to be spontaneous and to reproduce the ebbing and flowing rhythms of mood and feeling is not confined to single speeches, but gives coherence to extended episodes and to whole scenes. A well-known example is the scene at the Boar's-Head tavern in *1 Henry IV* (II. iv) immediately after the Gadshill robbery, when Falstaff invents his story of the four-seven-nine-eleven men in buckram, aided and abetted by the three men in Kendal green. This fine crescendo movement is followed a little later in the same scene by another piece of patterned action, when Falstaff impersonates the King and commends "a virtuous man whom I have often noted in thy company, but I know not his name", and then Falstaff impersonates Prince Hal, and the Prince, who has taken over the role of the King, warns him against "that villanous abominable misleader of youth, Falstaff, that old white-headed Satan". Equally well known is the quarrel between Brutus and Cassius in *Julius Caesar* (IV. iii), where the two men stand face to face exchanging verbal blows, each in turn catching up the words the other has just spoken and throwing them back at him, shouting angry question, interrupting, reiterating accusations, and so on:

> *Bru.*   You say you are a better soldier:
> Let it appear so; make your vaunting true,
> And it shall please me well: for mine own part,
> I shall be glad to learn of noble men.
> *Cas.*   You wrong me every way; you wrong me, Brutus;
> I said, an elder soldier, not a better:
> Did I say 'better'?
> *Bru.*   If you did, I care not.
> *Cas.*   When Caesar lived, he durst not thus have moved me.
> *Bru.*   Peace, peace! you durst not so have tempted him.
> *Cas.*   I durst not!
> *Bru.*   No.
> *Cas.*   What, durst not tempt him!
> *Bru.*   For your life you durst not. . . .

I have reserved for final discussion a passage in *Antony and Cleopatra* (V. ii. 71 ff.). Antony is dead: Cleopatra has already tried to destroy herself, and has only been prevented by Proculeius snatching the dagger from her hands. But she is now resolute for death, and is determined that the woman who loved and was loved by Antony shall never appear before the Roman populace to grace Caesar's triumph. At this point Dolabella enters, young, good-looking, and clearly prepared to make an impression upon Cleopatra:

> *Dol.*   Most noble empress, you have heard of me?
> *Cleo.*   I cannot tell.
> *Dol.*   Assuredly you know me.
> *Cleo.*   No matter, sir, what I have heard or known.
> You laugh when boys or women tell their dreams;
> Is't not your trick?
> *Dol.*   I understand not, madam.
> *Cleo.*   I dream'd there was an Emperor Antony;
> O, such another sleep, that I might see
> But such another man!

So far Cleopatra has acknowledged the presence of Dolabella; she has made some sort of answer to his questions, and has even noticed him so far as to ask him a question herself, although she is not going to be interested in any reply that he may make. But from now on Dolabella begins to fade from her field of consciousness; she is not thinking of this man, but of *her* man, Antony. What she has to say might have been given to us in the form of a long soliloquy; but Dolabella is there, and Shakespeare, who always seems to be fully aware of what any one of his characters is doing, or even how he will look at any given moment, sees a use for him. What might have been merely soliloquy becomes, therefore, something much more interesting: a closed reverie of the Queen into which Dolabella keeps trying to break. Three times he attempts to make his presence felt, and each time Cleopatra sweeps grandly past him. We are listening to a magnificent speech, and at the same time we are watching Cleopatra and Dolabella involved in a sort of mental ballet:

> *Dol.*   If it might please ye,—
> *Cleo.*   His face was as the heavens; and therein stuck
> A sun and moon, which kept their course, and lighted
> The little O, the earth.
> *Dol.*   Most sovereign creature,—
> *Cleo.*   His legs bestrid the ocean: his rear'd arm
> Crested the world: his voice was propertied
> As all the tuned spheres. . . .
>   . . . in his livery
> Walk'd crowns and crownets; realms and islands were
> As plates dropp'd from his pocket.
> *Dol.*   Cleopatra!
> *Cleo.*   Think you there was, or might be, such a man
> As this I dream'd of?
> *Dol.*   Gentle madam, no.
> *Cleo.*   You lie, up to the hearing of the gods.
> But, if there be, or ever were, one such,
> It's past the size of dreaming. . . .

The contrast between this new depth in Cleopatra and the well-bred shallowness of Dolabella, between the intense and absorbed queen and her uncomprehending auditor, gives us a sense of her tragic suffering that an unbroken soliloquy could hardly have produced. It is odd that Shakespeare, who very rarely repeats himself, should almost have done so here: in Act IV, scene iv, shortly before he falls upon his own sword, Antony is talking to Eros ("Sometimes we see a cloud that's dragonish . . ."), and in the "Ay, my lord" and "It does, my lord" of the puzzled Eros Shakespeare may be said to anticipate, more briefly, the Cleopatra-Dolabella situation. The effect in both cases is to lift the hero and heroine into a world of their own, a world into which the ordinary man cannot follow them. But the way in which Shakespeare achieves this is characteristic: it is the presence of Eros in the one scene and of Dolabella in the other that enables him to give to thought and feeling the shapely movement that increases their poignancy, and that makes us realize the spiritual point of no return that both Antony and Cleopatra have reached.

It would be wrong to suggest that the creative process I have been considering is not to be found in other dramatists and novelists; but it is nowhere so continuously present as it is in Shakespeare. More than any other writer he had the ability to enter fully into the minds and feelings of his characters, and into the situations in which they are placed, by virtue of a sympathy which amounts to almost complete identification of the dramatist with those creatures of his imagination. This will help to explain the apparent spontaneity of the dialogue in Shakespeare's plays. But behind the spontaneity, controlling it but never impeding it, lies this shaping power which I have tried to demonstrate, and which was, for Coleridge,[5] almost synonymous with the imagination—"this power, first put in action by the will and understanding, and retained under their irremissive, though gentle and unnoticed control", and revealing itself in "a more than usual state of emotion, *with more than usual order*".

NOTES

1. In quoting from the plays I have followed throughout the "Globe" edition of Shakespeare.
2. *Coleridge's Literary Criticism*, ed. J. W. Mackail (1908), p. 201. (*Table Talk*, 7 April 1833.)
3. *Ibid.* p. 202. (*Table Talk*, 5 March, 1834.)
4. *Shakespeare's Holinshed*, ed. W. G. Boswell-Stone (1896), p. 350.
5. *Biographia Literaria*, ed. J. W. Shawcross (1907), Vol. ii, p. 12.

Michael Jamieson

SHAKESPEARE'S CELIBATE STAGE

The Problem of Accommodation to the Boy-Actress
in *As You Like It, Antony and Cleopatra* and
*The Winter's Tale**

> The Characters of Women, on former Theatres, were perform'd by
> Boys, or young Men of the most effeminate Aspect. And what Grace, or
> Master-strokes of Action can we conceive such ungain Hoydens to have been
> capable of? This Defect was so well consider'd by *Shakespear*, that in few of
> his Plays, he has any greater Dependance upon the Ladies, than in the
> Innocence and Simplicity of a *Desdemona*, an *Ophelia*, or in the short
> Specimen of a fond and virtuous *Portia*.
>
> Colley Cibber,
An Apology for the Life of Mr. Colley Cibber, Comedian

> Much could be said for the restoring of the celibate stage; but the
> argument, one fears, would be academic.
>
> Harley Granville-Barker,
Prefaces to Shakespeare

A discussion like the present one, which is concerned less with literary
values than with stage practice, has to be conjectural in its method and
tentative in its conclusion. The theatre is—notoriously—ephemeral, a
fact on which certain of its chroniclers and remembrancers have impro-
vised that slow, sad, eschatological music which is typified by these
generalizations of Maurice Baring's:

> The actor's art dies with him; but the rumour of it, when it is very great,
> lives on the tongue and sometimes in the soul of man, and forms a part of his
> dreams and of his visions. The great of old still rule our spirits from their
> urns. . . . [1]

---

* This is a slightly revised version of a term-paper written some years ago for Professor
G. E. Bentley's graduate-course on Shakespeare (English 525) at Princeton University.
The subject needs fuller treatment, W. Robertson Davies's *Shakespeare's Boy Actors*
(London, 1939) being somewhat perfunctory. A glaring lack in my paper is shared by
Davies's book-length study—there is no comparison of Shakespeare's practice with other
Elizabethan and Jacobean playwrights' handling of their female roles, both in plays
written for the King's Men and in plays for other companies.

> The most enduring monuments, the most astounding miracles of beauty
> achieved by the art and craft of man, are but as flotsam, drifting for a little
> while upon the stream of Time; and with it now there is a strange russet leaf,
> the name of Sarah Bernhardt.[2]

The art of the Elizabethan boy-actresses, unlike that of Bernhardt, may not have been 'very great', and the rumours which have been preserved, both of their art and of their lives, are confused and scanty. My purpose is to discuss the effects, as far as they are still discoverable, which the enforced presence of boy-actresses in the Lord Chamberlain's/King's Men had on Shakespeare's presentation of women in three plays—*As You Like It*, *Antony and Cleopatra* and *The Winter's Tale*. I am not concerned with the child-actors, who played *all* the parts—boys, women, and old men[3]—in such companies as the Children of the Chapel, but with those few boys in the adult companies who specialized in women's parts and for whom Granville-Barker coined the useful term 'the boy-actress'.[4] To speak at this stage of Shakespeare's 'accommodation' to the boy-actress would be to beg the question, and I make no such initial assumption. What my approach does assume—and it is no longer revolutionary[5]—is that William Shakespeare, as housekeeper, company-sharer, actor, and dramatist-in-ordinary to his company, planned his plays with his fellow-actors constantly in mind for the parts he was writing, and that his views of their capabilities conditioned the parts as they survive today.

Plays are complex mechanisms, and a speech, a device, or a situation which seems, at first glance, to have a *theatrical* origin may, in fact, owe its existence to a literary tradition or may have been present already in Shakespeare's source. C. E. Montague, for instance, showed theatrical perception when he wrote:

> In the 'seven ages' speech in *As You Like It* you see Shakespeare meeting the
> technical difficulty that Orlando has just gone off to fetch Adam, and that
> something or other must be done to give him time to reach Adam and
> come back; you see Shakespeare timing the action, watch in hand as it
> were . . .

So far, excellent; but Montague proceeded:

> and possibly giving man an extra age or two, lest Orlando and Adam
> should seem to come incredibly soon.[6]

These last words altogether overlook the fact that the Seven—not Five or Six—Ages of Man was a commonplace of medieval philosophy. In trying to discover what effects the presence of boy-actresses had on Shakespeare's presentation of his women, a critic has to be cautious. *As You Like It*, *Antony and Cleopatra*, and *The Winter's Tale* represent three Shakespearean *genres*, comedy, tragedy, and romance, and between them they give a wide range of Shakespearean women, but a further reason for selecting these plays is that each has a single and unusually full source in Thomas Lodge, Sir Thomas North, and Robert Greene respectively. Shakespeare can thus be glimpsed in the process of adapting material for the stage, and one aspect of his dramaturgy, his presentation of women, can be studied in detail.

It would be possible to proceed directly to the three plays and make (rash) deductions about the boy-actress from them, but, mindful of Miss Bradbrook's warning that 'there is little that can be directly inferred from the plays about the style of acting at the Globe',[7] I find it necessary to decide, at some length, from slight contemporary references, quaint rumours, and sound scholarship, just which assumptions can legitimately be held about the boy-actress as the only solid basis for further deductions from the text.

I

What assumptions are we justified in making about the qualities of the boy-actresses who played Shakespeare's women? One set of notions was uncompromisingly stated by Sir Sidney Lee who, in 1906, wrote:

> In Shakespeare's day boys or men took the part of women, and how characters like Lady Macbeth and Desdemona were adequately rendered by youths beggars belief. But renderings in such conditions proved popular and satisfactory. Such a fact seems convincing testimony, not to the ability of Elizabethan or Jacobean boys—the nature of boys is a pretty permanent factor in human society—but to the superior imaginative faculty of adult Elizabethan or Jacobean playgoers.[8]

The Toryism of this Boys-will-be-boys view was challenged by George Pierce Baker in these words:

> Much of the current wonder that Shakespeare's heroines could have been adequately represented by boys and youths vanishes if one knows the contemporary evidence as to their exceeding skill and realises how long, thorough, and varied the training of an Elizabethan actor could be.[9]

Certainly Professor Baker, by directing students to contemporary testimony, is more illuminating than is Mr. Ronald Watkins, when, in an attempt to be helpful, he remarks:

> Anyone who has seen *Poil de Carotte*, . . . *Shoe Shine* or *The Fallen Idol* will be ready to believe that the acting of the Globe boys was not the least moving part of the performance . . . ,[10]

a modern analogy which is false on at least five counts, since in these films (a) *young* boys were playing *boys of their own ages* within (b) a convention of realistic acting and in (c) a non-continuous performance later given continuity in a cutting-room, with (d) directors of genius—Duvivier, de Sica, Reed—constantly at their sides engaged in (e) the most mechanised and easily-faked medium of artistic expression. Filmgoers who imagined in 1948 that young Master Bobby Henrey was consciously acting in *The Fallen Idol* should consult his fond mother's record of Sir Carol Reed's directorial chicanery, *A Film Star in Belgravia*. In recent years schoolmaster-producers like Mr. Watkins and Mr. Guy Boas have published records [11] of their own successful productions of Shakespeare's plays with schoolboy casts, tacitly suggesting that these performances have more nearly recaptured Shakespearian acting conditions than have those of the professional theatre. But it is one thing for a schoolboy Lady Macbeth to hold his own with a Macbeth from the Sixth Form, quite another for a trained boy-actress to play, on a weekly roster, the great women's roles of Shakespeare and of his fellow playwrights for the King's Men, professionally harnessed to a star-actor, Burbage, who was thirty-three [12] when he created Macbeth in 1605-6 and who relinquished the part only at his early death. I do not mean to disparage school performances of Shakespeare, but I suspect that their real purpose is to broaden the children's interests rather than to enable the masters who direct the productions to make scholarly points. Occasionally, of course, a gifted boy may give a performance of Portia or Katherina which is striking enough to refute as jaundiced a view of juvenile acting as Sir Sidney Lee's. Of Master Laurence Olivier's performance as Kate in a school production of *The Taming of the Shrew* in 1922, when he was fifteen, Dame Ellen Terry wrote in her diary:

> This gives us an idea of what the boy-actors in Shakespeare's time were like, yet people assume they were clumsy hobbledehoys.[13]

In general, however, to accept the phenomenon of juvenile amateur acting as anything but a shaky analogy for Elizabethan practice would be to ignore the essential issues of long training, established acting style, and professional disciplines which are involved.

It is not only the attitude of boys to acting which has changed, but that of an audience to the notion of such acting, so that where, by some trick of stage history, professional boy-actresses made a late survival, the Elizabethan attitude could never be recaptured. In 1788 Goethe saw a performance in Italy of Goldoni's *La Locandiera* in which men played the women's parts. Professor Nagler, in reprinting his reactions, suggests an analogy with the responses of Shakespeare's audience:

> After the initial strangeness had disappeared, Goethe experienced the unique aesthetic pleasure which Elizabethan playgoers must have felt when they watched boys playing Juliet and Cressida.[14]

It is significant, however, that the performance prompted Goethe to this philosophical discussion on the nature of theatrical illusion:

> I found [at the Roman comedies] a pleasure to which I had hitherto been a stranger. . . . in the particular kind of representation we witnessed, the idea of imitation, the thought of art was called forth vividly, and . . . only a kind of self-conscious illusion was produced.
>
> We . . . experience a double charm from the fact that these people are not women, but play the part of women. We see a youth who has studied the idiosyncrasies of the female sex in their character and behaviour; he has learned to know them, and reproduces them as an artist; he plays not himself, but a third, and in truth, a foreign nature.[15]

The performance *was* analogous to an Elizabethan one, but Goethe's attitude was sophisticated; he was over-conscious of 'the thought of art'. What he enjoyed was akin to the Brechtian alienation-effect. That 'initial strangeness' differentiates him from the Elizabethans; and one wonders if what worked for comedy would, in Goethe's late day, have worked for tragedy also.

The Elizabethan practice of casting boys in women's parts was a theatrical convention like any other; more serious, for instance, than that of British pantomime, where the Principal Boy is a strapping and obvious girl and the Dame is a red-nosed comedian in skirts, less rigid and rarified than the dynastic mysteries of female impersonation practised by gentlemen of Peking like Mr. Mei Lan-fang. The measure of a convention is that it goes unquestioned, so that Thomas Coryat recorded the shock, both moral and aesthetic, of seeing this convention shattered by foreigners. Of a Venetian theatre visit of 1608, he wrote:

> Here I observed certaine things that I never saw before. For I saw women acte, a thing that I never saw before, . . . and they performed it with as good a grace, action, gesture, and whatsoever convenient for a Player, as ever I saw any masculine Actor.[16]

Coryat seemed quite content with the way things were ordered in England: his highest praise of Italian actresses is that they were as good as English boys. This impression of the quality of Shakespeare's boy-actresses is reinforced by such stray allusions as Ingine's speech in *The Devil is an Ass* [17] in which he mentions the boy Richard Robinson passing as a woman at a gossips' feast,[18] but critical comments on boy-actresses came at a later, better-documented period of stage history. In two passages Pepys refers to female impersonations by the last of the boy-actresses, Edward Kynaston (born 1640?),[19] the only boy-actress whose portrait survives[20]:

> (a) *August 18, 1660.* [Saw] 'The Loyall Subject,' where one Kinaston, a boy, acted the Duke's sister, but made the loveliest lady that ever I saw in my life, *only her voice not very good.*[21]

(Some scholars who have reproduced this passage have omitted the last six words to avoid the question of Kynaston's poor voice, but by Miss McAfee's reckoning, Kynaston, whose training in the clandestine theatricals of the interregnum must have been spasmodic, would have been around twenty by this time, and, in more normal circumstances, would have graduated from women's parts by then. There is no reason for supposing Elizabethan boy-actresses' voices were poor, or that they habitually acted women's roles once their voices had broken. Hamlet and the players threatened by the Closing of the Theatres knew the value of a boy-actress's voice.)

> (b) *January 7, 1660-61.* Among other things here [in *The Silent Woman*], Kinaston, the boy, had the good turn to appear in three shapes: first, as a poor woman in ordinary clothes, to please Morose; then in fine clothes as a gallant, and in them was clearly the prettiest woman in the whole house, and lastly, as a man; and then likewise did appear the handsomest man in the house.[22]

Praise of Kynaston appears more authoritatively in a passage by John Downes in which that retired prompter attributes 'several', and by name four, women's parts to Kynaston who (he adds):

> ... being then very Young made a Compleat Female Stage Beauty, performing his Parts so well, especially *Arthiope* and *Aglaura*, being Parts greatly moving Compassion and Pity; that it has since been Disputable among the Judicious, whether any Woman that succeeded him so Sensibly touch'd the Audience as he.[23]

It is tempting to take at face value a passage from a play of 1676 which contains the line "Besides I can never endure to see Plays since Women came on the Stage; Boys are better by half," [24] but, in the context of the play,[25] it is clear that the speaker Snarl (an 'old pettish fellow, a great Admirer of the last Age and A Declaimer against the Vices of this, and privately very vicious himself') is a fault-finding hypocrite whose nostalgia is meant to carry no critical weight.

There is one kind of contemporary evidence which suggests that the Jacobean boy-actresses were effeminate. Puritan pamphleteers unleashed unambiguous accusations of homosexual relations between the boys and the adult players,[26] but gossip, to be credited, must have proven grounds, and such hysterical statements by Zeal-of-the-Land Busies cannot be checked at this date.

What we know of the organization and training of Elizabethan boy-actresses is sufficient to indicate that Kynaston was no solitary phenomenon. Boys joined the company under arrangements analogous to apprenticeship [27] from the age of ten upward [28]; they probably played first children's, then women's parts; each was boarded out with a company-sharer or hired-man who was responsible for the boy's further training.[29] Thus, although the acting life of each boy-actress must have been relatively short,[30] each was highly trained in speech, movement, music (if he had a voice), and in such arts as fencing which would equip him for an adult career, should he prove worthy, in his company. The stiff, brocaded, highly decorous costume of the Elizabethan lady may have contributed to successful female impersonation, but boy-actresses also had to play less decorously clad women like Doll Tearsheet and Dol Common. This is not the place to review scholarly debate on the nature of Elizabethan acting. The Elizabethans freely mingled extreme conventionalism and extreme realism in dramatic writing. Doubtless they did so in their acting, though it is safe to say that Elizabethan acting would seem formal by present-day standards. Indeed Professor Harbage has found in the success of the boy-actresses a further clue to Elizabethan acting style:

> My explanation of the apparent adequacy of the Elizabethan boy-actor is simply *formal acting*.[31]

The qualities Coryat commended in the British boy-actresses—*grace, action, gesture and whatsoever* [is] *convenient for a player* [32]—may seem odd alongside truth to life, spontaneity, conviction, or the concepts of Stanislavski or

Mr. Lee Strasberg, but they were probably among the criteria by which Shakespeare's boy-actresses were judged in the parts he wrote for them. Shakespeare's one revealing comment on the problem of the boy-actress's short career, Hamlet's lines—

> What, my yong Lady and Misstris? Byrlady your Ladiship is neerer Heauen then when I saw you last, by the altitude of a Choppine. Pray God your voice like a peece of vncurrant Gold be not crack'd within the ring.[33]

chimes exactly and sympathetically with the old stagers' professional concern voiced, at the time of the Closing of the Theatres, in *The Actors Remonstrance*:

> Our boyes, ere wee shalle have libertie to act againe, will be growne out of use, like crackt organ-pipes and have faces as old as our flags.[34]

In the three plays themselves, the basis for deciding the questions of Shakespeare's accommodation to his juvenile interpreters must be this image of the boy-actress as a youthful, highly trained, assured, and valuable performer, who, in stature and still-unbroken voice, would contrast effectively with the adult members of the Shakespearian company.

II

Of the three plays *The Winter's Tale* makes the simplest demands of the boy-actresses and, disregarding chronology, I take this late play first. The play has one star part, Leontes, whose 682 lines [35] went possibly to Burbage, and a group of important subsidiary roles, three of which, Paulina (325), Hermione (207), Perdita (128), required boy-actresses. The divided action of the play made doubling peculiarly feasible. Mamillius and the ladies of the court could be doubled with Mopsa, Dorcas, and other shepherdesses; it is possible that Mamillius and Perdita, in the interests of a family likeness, were played by one boy, and that the boys who played Hermione and Paulina 'walked on' as shepherdesses in the sheepshearing interlude. Thus the play met the basic requirement of the King's Men—it did not tax the numerical strength of their boy-actresses.[36] Of the important characters not in Greene's novel [37]—Antigonus, the Young Shepherd, Autolycus, Paulina—only one is a woman, and this new character was not a dramatic indulgence on Shakespeare's part, but the second character in the play and the one through whom Shakespeare effected and made credible the one significant deviation from his source, the resurrection of Hermione from cold storage which closes the play.

The *genre* to which this work belongs was indicated by John Donne, who once spoke in a sermon of the Book of Job as 'a representation of God in a Tragique-Comedy, *lamentable beginnings comfortably ended*'.[38] Shakespeare,

by plunging straight into such lamentable beginnings, seems to have
required of the boy-actress playing Hermione the simplest effects, which—
on a stage dominated by the insanely jealous Leontes—would have been
the more telling in dignity and calm:

> I must be patient, till the Heauens looke
> With an aspect more fauorable. Good my Lords,
> I am not prone to weeping (as our Sex
> Commonly are) . . . [39]

a speech which would have helped the boy-actress unemphatically to
establish Hermione's womanliness. The hobbledehoy theory [40] is belied
by Hermione's advanced pregnancy which (though Elizabethan costume
might preclude its representation) is graphically pointed out by Leontes:

> . . . and let her sport her selfe
> With that shee's big-with, for 'tis *Polixenes*
> Ha's made thee swell thus. [41]

in lines which would have defeated an inadequate boy-actress. All that is
asked of Hermione in the Trial is ringing sincerity ("Sir,/You speake a
Language that I vnderstand not": [42]) and a spectacular faint at the news
of Mamillius' death. She does not re-appear until, in the play's 'comfort-
able ending', the boy-actress, made up as an older woman and splendidly
dressed, was ceremonially revealed in a statuesque silent pose well within
his abilities.

The part of Paulina, that female Kent, is spiritedly conceived along
outspoken lines. Her function is primarily that of observer, commentator,
and critic. It is Paulina who opposes Leontes, who refuses to be silenced:

> *Pau.*   Let him that makes but trifles of his eyes
> First hand me. . . [43]

who too accusingly announces Hermione's death ("Alas, I haue shew'd
too much/The rashnesse of a woman: He is toucht/To th' Noble heart."[44]),
who brings the king to repentance, and who, in a double sense, stage-
manages the ceremonial reconciliation:

> *Pau.*   Musick; awake her: Strike:
> 'Tis time: descend: be Stone no more: approach:
> Strike all that looke vpon with meruaile[45]:

an invocation which demands impressive delivery by the boy-actress, just
as her would-be exit line demands graciousness:

> . . . I (an old Turtle)
> Will wing me to some wither'd bough, and there
> My Mate (that's neuer to be found againe)
> Lament, till I am lost.[46]

Paulina, despite her occasional shrewishness and even violence, personifies
loyalty and commonsense, and the part would have fitted the capacities
of a boy.

Perdita, the play's romantic heroine, is no realistic shepherdess. She makes a late and highly formal entrance, symbolically dressed as the goddess of flowers and fertility, to this accompanying speech of Florizel's:

> *Flo.* These your vnvsuall weeds, to each part of you
> Do's giue a life: no Sheperdesse but *Flora*
> Peering in Aprils front.[47]

The love-plot is presented, not through amorous action, but in such poetry as this transfiguration of the original meeting in the novel[48]:

> *Flo.* I blesse the time
> When my good Falcon, made her flight a-crosse
> Thy Fathers ground.[49]

or Florizel's:

> When you do dance, I wish you
> A waue o' the Sea, that you might euer do
> Nothing but that.[50]

Perdita's formal distribution of the flowers is part of a design through which the flower-freshness of the heroine is suggested. Here, as so often in Shakespeare, the verse when well-spoken does its own work upon an audience, and a trained boy-actress would have paired well here with an older boy as Florizel.

In Bohemia, Perdita and Florizel dominate the serious action. In the reconciliations and recoveries of the final act Perdita is mostly silent and an onlooker (which explains how a nineteenth-century stage beauty contrived to play Hermione *and* Perdita, with a stand-in for Act v), while Paulina controls and directs the scene in which the statue of Hermione warms to life.

Shakespeare's presentation of this trio of women, the two mature ladies of the court and the foundling-princess, accords well with the conventional assumptions of vivacity, skill, and subordination to an adult male player which are made about Shakespeare's boy-actresses.

III

A reading of *As You Like It*, however, forces a reconsideration of this conception of the boy-actress's task as subordinate (*a*) because in Rosalind Shakespeare gave the boy-actress twice as many lines (747) [51] as any other character in the play, and made the part, moreover, twice as long as that of Viola, and markedly longer than either Macbeth (704) or Prospero (665); and (*b*) because the virtuosity of Rosalind's two-fold impersonation within the play seems to have assumed a virtuosity in the original boy-actress.

Rosalind and Celia belong, with Portia and Nerissa, Beatrice and Hero, Viola and Olivia, to a series of paired heroines in which the first, the taller, takes the initiative while the second is placid and conventional. The text of *As You Like It*, following Lodge's novel,[52] confirms this physical contrast, on which indeed, is based the disguise—the woman as page—which Rosalind adopts for most of the play's action:

> *Ros.* Were it not better,
> Because that I am more then common tall,
> That I did suite me all points like a man ... [53]

This led Granville-Barker to point out what has become a cliché in discussions of this play, that 'through three-parts of the play a boy [as opposed to a modern actress] would have the best of it'.[54] This judgment I accept with considerable reserve. If, as commentators more ingenuous than Barker imply, Shakespeare's frequent recourse to this device of disguise was dictated by a need to put at ease his inadequate boy-actress (whose daily business, I would object, was female impersonation), how was the boy-actress first to impose himself on the audience as a great lady? Certainly a boy Rosalind would have made a more credible Ganymede and have justified Phoebe's infatuation, but Shakespeare did not use this device for purposes of credibility. Rosalind's essential femininity is revealed through (not in spite of) this disguise with such delicacy and dramatic skill that, in his fully documented examination of forty contemporary English plays containing the female page, Dr. Freeburg did not seem to find a subtler exploitation of this then-prevalent device.[55] Shakespeare and the boy-actress had therefore a technical problem which no woman Rosalind would have, for, the moment an audience accepts Ganymede *as a boy*, instead of as a credibly disguised woman, the drily romantic irony of Rosalind's scenes with Orlando evaporates. A convention of fairly formal acting and the unquestioning acceptance of the boy-actress (by which a regular playgoer could presumably say to himself "That's the woman" just as, looking at Kempe, he could say "That's the funny man") made this evaporation less likely, but, once Rosalind was disguised, Shakespeare's concern was constantly to stress that femininity breaks through Rosalind's strident (and on the Elizabethan stage possibly *too* manly) pose.

This femininity Shakespeare stressed in three ways. First, he made a comic theatrical point of Rosalind's falling short of that pose in such speeches as this:

> *Ros.* I could finde in my heart to disgrace my mans apparell, and to cry like a woman: but I must comfort the weaker vessell, as doublet and hose ought to show it selfe coragious to petty-coate; therefore courage, good *Aliena.*[56]

or the dialogue following Rosalind's faint at the sight of the napkin stained with Orlando's blood:

> *Oli.* Be of good cheere youth: you a man?
> You lacke a mans heart. ...[57]
> Well then, take a good heart, and counterfeit to be a man.
> *Ros.* So I doe: but yfaith, I should haue beene a woman by right.[58]

Secondly, Shakespeare fully exploited the passive Celia as confidant—
Rosalind's scenes with her are revealingly girlish, and in them she constantly speaks of herself *as a woman*:

> ... dost thou think though I am caparison'd like a man, I haue a doublet
> and hose in my disposition? [59]

Later in this scene Rosalind, on learning of Orlando's presence, stresses
her assumed boy's clothes four times in some seventy lines of the First
Folio text:

(a) *Ros.* Alas the day, what shall I do with my doublet & hose?[60]
(b) *Ros.* But doth he know that I am in this Forrest, and in man's
apparrell? [61]
(c) *Ros.* Do you not know I am a woman, when I thinke, I must
speake.[62]
(d) *Ros.* I wil speake to him like a sawcie Lacky, and vnder that habit play
the knaue with him.[63]

And after the mock love-scenes, it is to Celia that Rosalind's genuine
involvement is revealed in the excited and infectious speech:

> *Ros.* O coz, coz, coz: my pretty little coz, that thou didst know how many
> fathome deepe I am in loue: but it cannot bee sounded ... [64]

Thirdly, the essentially feminine Rosalind was depicted in those scenes
with Orlando in which the complex *theatrical* situation was that of a boy-
actress playing a girl, Rosalind, who, while disguised as a boy, Ganymede,
openly mimics herself in his character. Shakespeare at the outset cunningly
suggested to his audience the close association of boys and women ("for
the most part, cattle of this colour" [65]) and contrived to show both
Ganymede's impersonation of Rosalind and the real woman:

> *Orl.* But will my *Rosalind* doe so?
> *Ros.* By my life, she will doe as I doe.[66]

A Bradleian critic would argue (rightly) that such glimpses of the
female in the male as Rosalind's faint are psychologically true. They are
also, in the acted context of the play, theatrically necessary. They represent
a conscious, and successful, attempt by Shakespeare to ensure that
Rosalind's virtuosity steadily advances the play's romantic action. In
scenes of comedy, confidences, and unorthodox courtship, Shakespeare
anticipated, and compensated for, a boy's shortcomings and, by exploiting
his advantages, planned the part so that it could be played by a boy and
yet not lose its womanliness. The other women in this play are conventional
and minor characters, but of all the Shakespearian women who disguise
as pages, Rosalind, more than Viola, more than Imogen, more even than
Portia, is Shakespeare's gesture of faith in the boy-actress. What happens
at the end of *As You Like It* confirms this view. Nothing comparable
happens elsewhere in Shakespeare; and I do not recall parallels in other
plays of the period. The play ends on a daring break with tradition, as
Rosalind comes forward:

> *Ros.* It is not the fashion to see the Ladie the Epilogue: but it is no
> more vnhandsome, then to see the Lord the Prologue.

and her farewell to the audience reveals that essential pretence on which all boy-actresses' performances were based:

> *If I were a Woman*, I would kisse as many of you as had beards that pleas'd me, complexions that lik'd me, and breaths that I defi'de not: And I am sure, as many as have good beards, or good faces, or sweet breaths, will for my kind offer, when I make curt'sie, bid me farewell.   *Exit.*[67]

It is the cue for the boy-actress, as star of this comedy, to take a solo 'curtain'.

IV

If depicting Rosalind in terms of the boy-actress's ability was a challenge to Shakespeare, what of Cleopatra? His handling of this great part might itself be the subject of a single paper. Once more there is the simple problem of sheer length—Cleopatra's 670 lines come second only to Antony's 813, which makes her part formidable, but the disposition of the scenes makes the part more demanding than is Antony's since (*a*) within the divided worlds of Rome and Egypt Cleopatra has no physical part in the Roman scenes, and (*b*) once Antony is dead, the whole of Act v with the great climax of the play's ending—the high-water mark of Shakespeare's dramatic poetry—had to be borne by the boy-actress alone, a signal assumption of authority in that unknown player. Yet critics have expressed their amazement, not at the theatrical assumptions which lie behind such apportioning and emphasis, but at the very idea that *any* boy-actress *ever* attempted the part. Sir Sidney Lee recorded his incensed feelings on this matter thus:

> *It seems almost sacrilegious* to conceive the part of Cleopatra, the most highly sensitised in its minutest details of all dramatic portrayals of female character,—*it seems almost sacrilegious* to submit Cleopatra's sublimity of passion to interpretation by an unfledged representative of the other sex.[68]

It was with overcoming prejudices such as these that Granville-Barker was concerned in that part of his preface in which he developed the following argument:

> Shakespeare's Cleopatra had to be acted by a boy, and this did everything to determine, *not his view of the character, but his presenting of it.*[69]

This antithesis of view and presentation is admirable, but, it seems to me, that Barker, who saw the play as 'a tragedy of sex without one single scene of sexual appeal' [70] containing a maximum of three embraces, a play in which 'the best evidence . . . of Cleopatra's physical charms' is 'a description of them by . . . the misogynist Enobarbus—given us, moreover, at a time when she has been out of our sight for a quarter of an hour or so',[71] took minimal account certainly of both the attested competence of boy-actresses and the formalism of their acting, and possibly also of Shakespeare's complex response to Plutarch.[72]

The part of Cleopatra, in variety of mood, makes exhausting demands on its interpreter. Even within the conventions of Elizabethan acting, the part must have demanded temperament in its performer. Cleopatra is not merely regal. She must be, by turns, ferocious ("Ile vnhaire thy head" [73]), bawdy ("I take no pleasure/In ought an Eunuch ha's" [74]), brilliantly malicious (the superb, instantaneous dismissal of Octavia as "dull of tongue, and dwarfish" [75]), utterly feminine in impulse ("If you finde him sad,/Say I am dauncing" [76]). She must both match Antony's "You haue been a boggeler euer" [77] and rise to the great keening speeches at his death:

> Oh wither'd is the Garland of the Warre,
> The Souldiers pole is falne: young Boyes and Gyrles
> Are leuell now with men: The oddes is gone,
> And there is nothing left remarkeable
> Beneath the visiting Moone.[78]

Cleopatra, as Granville-Barker has shown, is frequently presented through the speeches of others (notably Enobarbus), but, in overstating the inferences from this fact, Barker suggested, perhaps unconsciously, that *tact* is Shakespeare's most conspicuous accommodation in this play. If physical embraces were embarrassing—though it is impossible now to know what Burbage did on the words "the Noblenesse of life/Is to do thus . . ." [79]— how was a boy-actress expected to bring off the scene in which Cleopatra seems to smother the dying Antony in kisses:

> Dye when thou hast liu'd,
> Quicken with kissing: had my lippes that power,
> Thus would I weare them out.[80]

The boy-actress had to back up the poetic allusions to Cleopatra's allure ("this great Fairey" [81]) not contradict them. What Plutarch—or North— called Cleopatra's flickering enticement is suffused throughout the speeches of the play, as is Antony's god-like stature, in images which, with the persistence of a leitmotif in opera, raise the standing of Antony and Cleopatra as persons tragically involved in the play's action. These allusions to the legendary Cleopatra are both a booster to the boy-actress and an indication of how greatly Shakespeare, engaged in the necessary compressions of dramatizing his source, was imaginatively stimulated by Plutarch. They are dramatically necessary because Cleopatra is uniquely incapable of a full representation on the stage, as Miss Tallulah Bankhead, Miss Vivien Leigh, Miss Katharine Hepburn, and other glamorous actresses have discovered in our own day, not because an embarrassed boy-actress was basically inadequate.

The inspired solo of the play's end reinforces this. Shakespeare clearly had great confidence in his boy-actress to have given him, in the deeply serious scene in which Cleopatra resolves on suicide, the daring lines:

> . . . and I shall see
> Some squeaking *Cleopatra* Boy my greatnesse
> I'th' posture of a Whore.[82]

While the psychology of the Elizabethan playgoer was such that the boy-actresses were accepted without question, this deliberate reminder, which has no precedent in Plutarch, would, on the lips of an inadequate or awkward boy, be a fatal preparation for the ceremony of purification which follows:

> I am Fire, and Ayre; my other Elements
> I giue to baser life.[83]

And how (to overstate the case) could a blushing, embarrassed, flat-chested boy carry that penultimate speech:

> *Cleo.* Peace, peace:
> Dost thou not see my Baby at my breast,
> That suckes the Nurse asleepe.[84]

Shakespeare used devices of imagery and rhetoric in an essentially dramatic way, seizing on every suggestion he found in Plutarch, to make Cleopatra playable on the Jacobean stage, but, in accommodating himself to the boy-actress, he did not sacrifice a single emotional effect.

V

Shakespeare's texts, as they survive, are a guide to his theatrical intentions and to the artistic effects which were available to him, but play-scripts, especially those in which stage-directions are few, can be a tantalizingly incomplete record of the original performances. A discussion like the present one is really concerned not only with what Shakespeare did as a writer, but what he did as a producer also—not only with the words he gave the actors of his company (over whom he had, for a dramatist, special authority) but with how he wanted them to speak, to move, to express emotion. Since our knowledge of the Elizabethan theatre, and of techniques of acting and of presentation there, is incomplete and based in part on conjecture, conclusions have to be tentative. What effects, then, of the presence of the boy-actress are still discernible in the women's parts as they survive today?

These three plays do not give a fully representative cross-section of Shakespearean women, but a reading of them allows some valid generalization on the question of accommodation to the boy-actress. Shakespeare kept his cast of women small. He often planned women's parts to be brief also, less because his boy-actresses were inadequate than because the whole drift of Elizabethan drama, particularly in the history plays which were Shakespeare's dramatic apprenticeship, was virile. Ophelia and Lady Macbeth are supporting parts, not in accommodation to the boy-actress, nor even in deference to Burbage, but in accordance with Saxo-Grammaticus who was concerned with Hamlet and with Holinshed whose theme was Macbeth. It is true that there are aspects of female character which Shakespeare did not ask his boy-actresses to explore, but I cannot agree with Miss Margaret Webster who believes:

> It is easy to see *what Shakespeare refrained from doing* because of this limitation [the boy-actress], if such he considered it, but not so easy to define what *positive* effect it had on the great women's parts.[85]

The first part seems dangerously mistaken, because no one can ever know why Shakespeare chose *not* to do the things he did not do, or even that the question of choice arose. The lesson of *Antony and Cleopatra* is that when Shakespeare decided to tackle a tragedy of sexual infatuation, he achieved his aim within the capabilities of the boy-actress. It is difficult to define the positive effects of the boy-actress's presence, because a particular play so often shatters our limiting assumptions, but chief among these positive effects in the depiction of *young* women is an exploitation of the boy-actress's natural qualities of youth. In comedy, where Rosalind is the exemplar, Shakespeare drew on the boy's resources of gaiety, impudence, high spirits, fresh, ringing tones and youthful self-confidence and swagger. In tragedy or romance (Perdita is an incomplete example) he drew on complementary resources of innocence, openness of disposition, and an elusive selflessness. Such an explanation of the character of these women has been condemned by Professor Stoll as too mechanistic and materialistic[86]; it is not meant as a complete explanation.

Each of the women's parts, particularly the unconventional ones (which are never the first that the generic term 'Shakespearian Women', with its feminist overtones of Mrs. Jameson, brings to mind), posed its own problems in technique, exposition and accommodation, but the inference from Rosalind and Cleopatra is that once Shakespeare was aware what problems the boy-actress would have to face his view of the character remained unaltered and he denied himself no single legitimate effect in presenting his great succession of women on the celibate stage.

NOTES

1. Maurice Baring, *The Puppet Show of Memory* (London, 1922), p. 227.
2. Maurice Baring, *Punch and Judy* (London, 1924), p. 42.
3. Hence the image of the Parcae's mistake in Ben Jonson's epitaph for the thirteen-year-old Salomon or Solomon Pavy who 'acted old men so truly' that he was carried off long before his time. See Epigram CXX reprinted by C. H. Herford and Percy and Evelyn Simpson in *Ben Jonson* (Oxford, 1925-52), Vol. VIII, p. 77. This should not be taken to mean that boys ever played old men *in the adult companies*. See note 10, below.
4. Harley Granville-Barker, *Prefaces to Shakespeare*, First series (London, 1927), p. xxvii.

5. See, for instance, the 'placing' of Shakespeare by G. E. Bentley: '... of all the swarm of Elizabethan dramatists who made the English theatre great, Shakespeare is the one most intimately and continuously associated with actors and theatres. Actors were his professional colleagues and his daily associates.' *The Swan of Avon and the Bricklayer of Westminster* (Princeton, 1946), p. 6. Or Professor J. Dover Wilson's declaration that Shakespeare wrote 'not books but prompt-books, or, if you will, theatrical scores for the performance of moving pageants of speech, action, and colour, upon a particular stage by a particular troupe of actors for a particular audience'. Quoted (without reference) by Allardyce Nicoll, 'Studies in the Elizabethan Stage since 1900', *Shakespeare Survey*, I (Cambridge, 1948), p. 13.

6. *A Writer's Notes On His Trade* (London, 1930), pp. 229-30.

7. M. C. Bradbrook, *Elizabethan Stage Conditions* (Cambridge, 1932), p. 105.

8. Sidney Lee, *Shakespeare and the Modern Stage* (London, 1906), p. 19.

9. George Pierce Baker, *The Development of Shakespeare as a Dramatist* (New York, 1907), pp. 56-57.

10. Ronald Watkins, *On Producing Shakespeare* (London, 1950), p. 165. Mr. Watkins's film-list also includes *Mädchen in Uniform*. I fail to see the present relevance of this drama of Freudian growing pains in a Potsdam school for the daughters of impoverished officers. Mr. Watkins's basic point is the ability of children to express strong emotions. He might, more happily, have cited H. N. Hillebrand's study *The Child Actors* (Urbana, 1926), which shows the prevalence *in Shakespeare's own day* of juvenile acting in pageants, royal progresses, pre-Reformation church rituals, grammar- and choir-schools, and boys' companies. It was on this long-established tradition of juvenile acting that the professional theatres drew, rather than on vague capacities to express emotion.

11. Mr. Watkins described his production of *A Midsummer Night's Dream* (at Harrow) in *Moonlight at the Globe* (London, 1946), Guy Boas some surprising selections (*e.g. Troilus and Cressida*) for performance by the boys of the Sloane School, Chelsea, in *Shakespeare and the Young Actor* (London, 1955).

12. Burbage's age is discussed by Thomas Whitfield Baldwin, *The Organisation and Personnel of the Shakespearean Company* (Princeton, 1927), pp. 238-9.

13. *Ellen Terry's Memoirs*, ed. by Edith Craig and Christopher St. John (New York, 1932), p. 326.

14. A. M. Nagler, *Sources of Theatrical History* (New York, 1952), p. 433.

15. From *Goethe's Travels in Italy*, trans. Charles Nisbeth (London, 1883), pp. 569-70. Reprinted by Nagler, pp. 433-4.

16. *Coryat's Crudities* (London, 1611), p. 247. New edn. 2 vols. (Glasgow, 1905), Vol. I, p. 386.

17. Ben Jonson, *The Divell is an Asse*, II, viii, Herford-Simpson, *Ben Jonson* Vol. VI, p. 208.

18. Professor Harbage mentions that Robinson could 'pass as a woman off the stage,' and adds the warning 'but notice this is off the stage *on the stage*'. Alfred Harbage, 'Elizabethan Acting', *PMLA*, Vol. 54 (1939), p. 691, n. 15. The paper is reprinted in *Theatre for Shakespeare* (Toronto, 1955).

19. Conjectural date by Helen McAfee, *Pepys on the Restoration Stage* (New Haven, 1916), p. 225.

20. Mezz. pl., engraved by R. B. Parkes after R. Cooper, to Colley Cibber's *Apology*, 7th edn., ed. Lowe, 2 vols. (London, 1889), Vol. I, facing p. 122. Reproduced by W. Robertson Davies, *op. cit.*, my preliminary note.

21. McAfee, p. 225. Italics added.
22. McAfee, p. 225. But the part of Epicene makes this case of female impersonation a special one, a point well made in a letter to *The Times* of 22 February, 1909, reprinted—and attributed to William Poel—by the editors of the Oxford *Ben Jonson*, Vol. IX, p. 220, in which the correspondent [Poel?] insists that 'the essential thing is that the principal female character must be played by a boy or youth'.
23. John Downes, *Roscius Anglicanus* (London, 1708). New edn., ed. Montague Summers (London, n.d.), p. 19.
24. Thomas Shadwell, *The Virtuoso, a comedy acted at the Duke of York's Theatre* (London, 1676), Act I (p. 16). Reprinted, for biographical purposes, by Professor Bentley, *The Jacobean and Caroline Stage* (Oxford, 1941), Vol. II, p. 588, where, of course, no theatrical inference is drawn.
25. *Ibid.* 'Drammatis Personae', B 4ᵛ. See also Albert S. Borgman, *Thomas Shadwell: His Life and Comedies* (New York, 1928), pp. 163-4.
26. Passages from Philip Stubbs, Stephen Gosson and William Prynne are reprinted, and inconclusively discussed, by Davies, *op. cit.* pp. 9-18.
27. Professor Baldwin in *Organisation and Personnel*, pp. 32-33, argued that the boys 'would be taken under the provision of the apprentice law . . . (5 Eliz. c. 4)', but ignores the fact that, as there was no actors' guild, legal apprenticeship was impossible.
28. Baldwin, p. 35, leaned heavily towards ten as the entering age (which would square with his notions of an *actual* apprenticeship) but confessed that '. . . of eight *fairly* definite cases *one* apprentice entered at ten and five others *almost certainly* did; all were certainly taken *before they were thirteen*'. My italics emphasize the vagueness of the evidence Baldwin brought to his thesis.
29. Talk of master and boy survives in Wright's *Historia Histrionica* of 1699 in which Truman speaks of Hart as 'Robinson's Boy or Apprentice'. Reprinted by Bentley, *Jacobean and Caroline Stage* v. Vol. II, p. 692.
30. See Hamlet's speech and *The Actors Remonstrance* v, quoted p. 27.
31. Harbage, *op. cit.* (n. 18 above), p. 703. The case for extremely formal acting has been put by B. L. Joseph in *Elizabethan Acting* (London, 1951) and elsewhere. For a rebuttal of Joseph see J. F. Kermode in *Review of English Studies*, n.s. Vol. 4 (1953), pp. 70-73. See also S. L. Bethell, 'Shakespeare's Actors', *Review of English Studies* n.s. Vol. 1 (1950), pp. 193-205; R. A. Foakes, 'The Player's Passion: Elizabethan Psychology and Acting', *Essays and Studies*, n.s. Vol. 7 (1954), pp. 62-77; A. M. Nagler, *Shakespeare's Stage* (New Haven, 1958); Marvin Rosenberg, 'Elizabethan Actors: Men or Marionettes?', *PMLA*, Vol. 69 (1954), pp. 915-27. (A lecture-demonstration by Dr. Joseph and a band of players who visited the University of Sussex with him on 23 February, 1964, convinced me that I have misrepresented his views above, or that he has modified them. See the new edition of *Elizabethan Acting* just published.)
32. Coryat, quoted p. 25.
33. *Hamlet* II. ii. 444-9. Oo 4. Act, scene and line references are to G. L. Kittredge's one-volume edition (Boston, 1936). Signatures refer to the First Folio, against which spelling has been checked.
34. *The Actors Remonstrance, or Complaint for the silencing of their profession* (London, 1643). Reprinted by W. C. Hazlitt, *The English Drama and Stage under the Tudor and Stuart Princes 1543-1664* (London, 1869), p. 263.
35. The figures throughout are from Professor Baldwin's tables, *Organisation and Personnel*, between pp. 228 and 229.

36. 'From three to five boys would normally have been sufficient for the female parts.' E. K. Chambers, *William Shakespeare: A Study of Facts and Problems* (Oxford, 1930), Vol. I, p. 82.

37. *Pandosto. The Triumphe of Time* (London, 1588). Reprinted, *New Variorum Edition* (Philadelphia, 1898), pp. 324-52.

38. Sermon VII, St. Paul's, Christmas Day 1629. *Complete Poetry and Selected Prose*, ed. John Hayward (London, 1929), p. 592.

39. II. i. 106-9; Aa 3ᵛ.

40. See n. 13 above.

41. II. i. 60-62; Aa 3ᵛ.

42. III. ii. 80-81; Aa 6.

43. II. iii. 62-63; Aa 4ᵛ.

44. III. ii. 221-3; Aa 6ᵛ.

45. V. iii. 98-100; Cc 1ᵛ.

46. V. iii. 132-5; Cc 2.

47. IV. iv. 1-3; Bb 2.

48. '... Dorastus (who all that daye had bene hawking ...)' *Variorum*, p. 339.

49. IV. iv. 14-16; Bb 2.

50. IV. iv. 140-2; Bb 2ᵛ.

51. Baldwin's figures, between pp. 228 and 229.

52. *Rosalynde. Euphues golden legacie* (London, 1590). Reprinted, *New Variorum Edition* (Philadelphia, 1890), pp. 317-87.

53. I. iii. 116-18; Q 5. All other references to Rosalind's height agree with this, except one line of Le Beau's (I. ii. 283; Q 4ᵛ) in which Celia is described: "But yet indeede the taller is his daughter." This has led Professor Dover Wilson to argue in the New Cambridge edition of the play (Cambridge, 1926), p. 103, that in the first performances Rosalind was played 'by a short boy, shorter than the boy who played Celia' but that, in the later performances for which the text (as we have it) had been revised, Rosalind was played by a much taller boy—or by the same boy grown taller. The one word 'taller', which is a likely printer's error for 'smaller', hardly warrants such a theory—particularly as Rosalind's height is emphasized by Lodge: "I (thou seest) am of a tall stature, and would very well become the person and apparell of a page..." *Variorum*, p. 331,—but Professor Wilson's theory usefully reminds us that, even in Shakespeare's lifetime, a succession of boys must have played these parts in the stock company of the King's Men.

54. *Prefaces*, First series, p. xxvii.

55. Victor Oscar Freeburg, *Disguise Plots in Elizabethan Drama* (New York, 1915), pp. 98-99.

56. II. iv. 4-8; Q 6.

57. IV. iii. 164-5; R 6.

58. IV. iii. 174-7; R 6.

59. III. ii. 204-6; R 2ᵛ.

60. III. ii. 231-2; R 2ᵛ.

61. III. ii. 242-3; R 2ᵛ.

62. III. ii. 263-4; R 2ᵛ.

63. III. ii. 313-15; R 3.

64. IV. i. 209-11; R 5ᵛ.

65. III. iii. 434-5; R 3.

66. IV. i. 158-9; R 5.

67. [Epilogue] 1-3 and 19-25; S2. Italics added.

68. Sidney Lee, *op. cit.* (n. 8 above), p. 42. Italics added.

69. *Prefaces to Shakespeare*, Second Series (London, 1930), p. 203. Italics added.

70. *Prefaces*, First series, p. xxviii.
71. *Prefaces*, Second series, p. 204.
72. *Plutarch's Lives, translated out of French into English by Thomas North* (London, 1595). Abridged version of North's life of Antony, *New Variorum Edition* (Philadelphia, 1907), pp. 388-409.
73. II. v. 64; [x]x 4ᵛ.
74. I. v. 9-10; [x]x 2ᵛ.
75. III. iii. 19; [x]x 6ᵛ.
76. I. iii. 3-4; [x]x 1ᵛ.
77. III. xiii. 110; [y]y 3.
78. IV. xv. 64-68; [y]y 6-6ᵛ.
79. I. i. 36-37; vv 6ᵛ.
80. IV. xv. 38-40; [y]y 6.
81. IV. viii. 12; [y]y 4ᵛ.
82. V. ii. 219-21; zz 1ᵛ.
83. V. ii. 292-3; zz 2.
84. V. ii. 311-13; zz 2.
85. Margaret Webster, *Shakespeare Without Tears* (New York, 1942), p. 93.
86. E. E. Stoll, *Shakespeare's Young Lovers* (London, 1937), p. 54.

D. J. Gordon

NAME AND FAME:
SHAKESPEARE'S CORIOLANUS[1]

" estrangement between your name and you "

W. H. Auden

I

Name is Fame, is Honour, and is won by deeds; in Rome, by deeds in war.

> Now in those days, valliantnes [so North renders Plutarch] was honoured
> in Rome above all other vertues: which they called *Virtus*, by the name of
> vertue selfe, as including in that generall name all other speciall vertues
> besides.[2]

So Cominius the General in his formal encomium, his *laus* of Caius
Marcius, begins:

> It is held
> That valour is the chiefest virtue and
> Most dignifies the haver.[3]

We are shown the deeds of Coriolanus, and their rewarding in the field:
the garland, the horse, the name with the consenting acclamations.
Cominius proclaims:

> Therefore be it known,
> ... that Caius Marcius
> Wears this war's garland; in token of the which,
> My noble steed, known to the camp, I give him,
> With all his trim belongings; and from this time
> For what he did before Corioli call him
> With all th' applause and clamour of the host,
> Caius Marcius Coriolanus.
> Bear th' addition nobly ever![4]

Drums and trumpets sound and the gathered army shouts, in formal
acclamation:

> Caius Marcius Coriolanus!

Coriolanus enters Rome wearing the wreath, and a Herald proclaims:

> Know, Rome, that all alone Marcius did fight
> Within Corioli gates, where he hath won,
> With fame, a name to Caius Marcius; these
> In honour follows Coriolanus.
> Welcome to Rome, renowned Coriolanus![5]

And again there is formal acclamation by the city, people and patricians:

> Welcome to Rome, renowned Coriolanus.

And Volumnia says:

> My gentle Marcius, worthy Caius, and
> By deed achieving honour newly nam'd
> What is it, Coriolanus must I call thee? [6]

Those speeches Shakespeare did not find in North's Plutarch (in general it may be taken that what I am pointing to in Shakespeare is not in North: significant coincidences I shall indicate).

Honour as reward for virtue, as a motive for action, is taken for granted. So is our concern for self-perpetuation in futurity: it is to this that our procreation of children, our anxiety to continue our names, our practice of adoption, inscriptions on monuments, panegyrics, all testify—so Cicero says.[7] It is the name that endures. All this is so quietly assumed— Plutarch does so throughout—that it requires only formal statement: as by the women in their last appeal to Coriolanus to spare the City—and here Shakespeare has expanded and heightened his source—when his wife Virgilia speaks as one

> That brought you forth this boy to keep your name
> Living to time.[8]

and Volumnia recalls the existence and function of the historian:

> if thou conquer Rome, the benefit
> Which thou shalt thereby reap is such a name
> Whose repetition shall be dogg'd with curses;
> Whose chronicle thus writ: "The man was noble,
> But with his last attempt he wip'd it out,
> Destroy'd his country, and his name remains
> To th' ensuing age abhorr'd. . . ." [9]

Banished from Rome, Coriolanus makes his way to his and Rome's chief enemy, Aufidius the Volscian, enters his house in disguise, and with his head "muffled". This is from the source. But new is Coriolanus' dialogue with the servants, and with Aufidius when he is sent for:

> *Aufidius.*   . . . Thy name?
>   Why speak'st not? Speak, man. What's thy name?
> *Coriolanus [unmuffling].*   If, Tullus,
>   Not yet thou know'st me, and seeing me, dost not
>   Think me for the man I am, necessity
>   Commands me name myself.
> *Aufidius.*   What is thy name?
> *Coriolanus.*   A name unmusical to the Volscians' ears,
>   And harsh in sound to thine.
> *Aufidius.*   Say, what's thy name?
>   Thou hast a grim appearance, and thy face
>   Bears a command in't; though thy tackle's torn,
>   Thou show'st a noble vessel. What's thy name?
> *Coriolanus.*   Prepare thy brow to frown—know'st thou me yet?
> *Aufidius.*   I know thee not. Thy name? [10]

This leads up to the disclosure of the name, in a speech that follows North closely:

> *Coriolanus.*   My name is Caius Marcius, who hath done
>   To thee particularly, and to all the Volsces,
>   Great hurt and mischief; there to witness may
>   My surname, Coriolanus. The painful service,
>   The extreme dangers, and the drops of blood
>   Shed for my thankless country, are requited
>   But with that surname—a good memory
>   And witness of the malice and displeasure
>   Which thou shouldst bear me. Only that name remains:
>   The cruelty and envy of the people,
>   Permitted by our dastard nobles, who
>   Have all forsook me, hath devour'd the rest;
>   And suffered me by th' voice of slaves to be
>   Whoop'd out of Rome.[11]

In *Coriolanus*, as in the other two plays in which he is substantially concerned with the critique of Honour, *Henry the Fourth*, Part I and *Troilus and Cressida*, Shakespeare takes Honour won in war and sets it in relation to the civil life, seen as "the specialty of rule", which in all three plays is offered as "policy". Here its scope is within the city, Rome.

II

> ... by the voice of slaves to be
> Whoop'd out of Rome.

In a passage where Shakespeare has wished to assimilate and preserve the recorded words of history so faithfully, the smallest departure from his text marks an act of significant choice. His transformation of North's "let me be banished by the people" [12] is radical. Whooped is a trivial word: a whoop is a phatic gesture expressing what its context requires. It is rare in Shakespeare, and only here does he use it as part of a transitive verb. This weight augments the sense of its triviality; it cheapens those who use it and him it is used against. Itself meaningless, it is uttered by the voice of the people (that Shakespeare should make Coriolanus call them, here, slaves belongs to a story other than that I am telling now). What has made Shakespeare's play possible is the meanings of the word 'voice'.

Voice, *vox*, is what utters, and what is uttered, and also what is uttered in a special restricted and technical sense. This technical sense we translate as vote. It is what Hamlet means when he says of Fortinbras

> ... I do prophesy the election lights
> On Fortinbras, he has my dying voice.[13]

In the procedure of election to the Elizabethan House of Commons the first and often the only method was that by voice; this means in the first instance literally what it says, by utterance. The election was held at the County Court, presided over by the Sheriff. If there were more nominations than seats, then the electors shouted for their man, and the Sheriff had to decide who had more voices. Coriolanus is elected Consul by the voices of the people: the voices that whoop him have the technical meaning.

It is the word Shakespeare found in North; and North had it from Amyot's French, which he was following. Amyot uses *voix* to translate Plutarch's ψῆφος; or sometimes *voix et suffrages*. Amyot was accommodating the Roman to the French usage; and North [14] could take his word over because French *voix* and English voice coincided in their applications. Yet for the Englishman the meaning was more urgent: its immediate association with the turbulence of Elizabethan elections guaranteed that; and a curious point verifies the supposition. When it came to Coriolanus' final formal trial before the people, Plutarch describes how the Tribunes rigged the voting by arranging that it should be done not by centuries but by tribes, to guarantee a majority for the people. Amyot, thinking it necessary to explain how this worked, inserted a parenthesis in the text:

> à cause que les voix se comptaient par tête.[15]

North retained this and translated *tête* by *poll*:

> bicause their voyces were numbred by the polle.[16]

This is a highly technical phrase and brings Coriolanus right into the thick of a disputed English election. Numbering by the poll was the last resort—heads were counted as the qualified voters passed before the Sheriff or his officer. At this point, says Sir John Neale—whose account of procedure I have been following—"The lists compiled during the canvassing seem to have come in useful both for marshalling the voters and recording their names and their votes." [17] And it is this procedure that Shakespeare envisages when, before Coriolanus comes to face the people, he makes one of the Tribunes say to an Aedile—Sheriff's Officers, obviously—

> Have you a catalogue
> Of all the voices that we have procur'd,
> Set down by the poll?[18]

The word voice, then, in a flash, holds a past world and a present world together. Further, it is an active word, containing act, situation, what utters, the uttering as well as the significance of what is uttered. The degree of abstraction required to make it synonymous with vote, to separate that out from the act is high and could, I believe, only be achieved in a strictly controlled context. What is likely to happen is shown in a sentence Neale quotes from a letter written in 1614 by an anxious parent to a son about to stand for Parliament: " Your friends must not be spare-voiced, but with their voices pronounce it (i.e. his name) roundly and fully." [19] The tribune's meaning, controlled as it is by "catalogue", "procur'd" and "set down", is clearly closer to the neutral sense given in, say, an election writ. But Hamlet's lines have in them as well as the formal vote the physical act we watch, a man speaking in anguish in a death agony. Coriolanus' "by the voice of slaves" contains act and significance.

In Act ɪɪ scene iii Coriolanus, back from the wars in triumph, his surname formally pronounced, standing for the Consulship, the final honour that the city can bestow, must, as the custom is, stand in the Forum, wearing the napless vesture of humility, display his wounds, and ask the people for their voices. This word echoes through the scene. Formally, at the beginning: "if he do require our voices, we ought not to deny him", "Are you all resolv'd to give your voices? " With a sense of the act: "everyone of us has a single honour in giving him our own voices with our own tongues." On Coriolanus' lips, humiliated, frustrated, furious that he should come to this, the word is qualified mockingly: *good* voice, *sweet* voice, the *tune* of your voice, *worthy* voices—resentment at the power of what they say, of the uttering, and his need of it, expressed by the ironical assumption that it is the uttering itself that he is wooing and the people are their voices, personified voices. Here is the bitter climax of this episode:

> Here come moe voices.
> Your voices. For your voices I have fought;
> Watch'd for your voices; for your voices bear
> Of wounds two dozen odd; battles thrice six
> I have seen and heard of; for your voices have
> Done many things, some less, some more.
> Your voices?[20]

When the tribune speaks of "all the voices that we have procur'd", the use is quite technical and the abstraction is so complete that the sense of the act has quite gone; when Coriolanus says "Here come moe voices" we see the men; his synecdoche reduces their whole reality to this one function or attribute. This is supported by the assimilation of the people to the organs of speech. They are mouths, or tongues, in the heads that contain them, with a reference to the polls that are counted, and there are two inclusive references, to Hydra the monster with many heads, and to the anthropomorphic image of the body politic established by Shakespeare—however equivocal his purposes may be—in the first scene of the play when he makes Menenius retail, from Plutarch, the famous apologue of the belly and the other members of the body. From voice there are further stages. When the Tribunes pronounce the formal sentence of banishment Coriolanus turns on the people—the last time he speaks to them:

> You common cry of curs, whose breath I hate
> As reek o' the rotten fens. . . .[21]

From the human voice to the cry of animals. Not the cry of hounds, those noble and disciplined beasts, but of base-born and ill-conditioned curs.

With those lines compare Cominius and Menenius to the crowd when the news of Coriolanus' approach on the city has come:

> *Com.* Y'are goodly things, you voices!
> *Men.*   You have made
> Good work, you and your cry![22]

and, in the same scene, Menenius to the Tribunes:

> . . .you that stood so much
> Upon the voice of occupation and
> The breath of garlic-eaters![23]

Voice and breath need not be paralleled; voice is subsumed in breath.

> Not all the water in the rough rude sea
> Can wash the balm off from an anointed king;
> The breath of worldly men cannot depose
> The deputy elected by the Lord.[24]

In those famous lines from *Richard II* the passage voice/breath is clear; and so is the significance of reducing voice/vote to what it uses or is made of. Coriolanus pleads that he be not forced to expose his wounds

> As if I had received them for the hire
> Of their breath only.[25]

And the power, existence, of the mob is located in its stinking breath:

> Nor showing, as the manner is, his wounds
> To th' people, beg their stinking breaths.[26]

These are prologues to the banishment and election scenes; and it is to this that Coriolanus and Menenius return. And further, voice like *vox* has a technical sense in grammar: a voice means word, what is uttered, and the voice, utterance, that Coriolanus is asking for, is his name.

III

Let us start again, this time from a passage in one of Seneca's letters. He is trying to convince Lucilius that to argue for the worth of posthumous renown (*claritas*) does not contradict the view that there is no such thing as an extrinsic good. It is the opposition's arguments, as Seneca presents them, that concern us:

> "Dicitis", inquit, "nullum bonum ex distantibus esse? Claritas autem ista bonorum virorum secunda opinio est. Nam quomodo fama non est unius sermo nec infamia unius mala existimatio, sic nec claritas uni bono placuisse. Consentire in hoc plures insignes et spectabiles viri debent, ut claritas sit". . . . "Claritas", inquit, "laus est a bonis bono reddita; laus oratio, vox est aliquid significans; vox est autem, licet virorum sit bonorum, non bonum."

And, a moment later, he reiterates such objections:

> "Quid ergo", inquit, "et fama erit unius hominis existimatio et infamia unius malignus sermo?" "Gloriam quoque", inquit, "latius fusam intellego, consensum enim multorum exigit."

And, again:

> "Ad gloriam aut famam non est satis unius opinio."

And:

> "Sed laus", inquit, "nihil aliud quam vox est, vox autem bonum non est."[27]

All this Shakespeare's contemporary, Thomas Lodge, in 1614 rendered:

> Thou wilt say, You other Stoicks maintaine that no good is composed of things distant. But this glorie whereof we entreat, is a fauourable opinion of good men. For as a good fame is not one man's words, neither infamy one mans misreport: so is it not praise to please one good man, many famous and worthy men must consent herein to make it glorie. . . . glorie (saith he) is a commendation given by good men to a good man: commendation is a speech, a speech is a voice that signifieth something. But the voice, although it be a good mans voice, is not goodnesse. . . .

and:

> What then (saith he) shal fame depend vpon the estimate of one man, and infamie be tied to the mis-report of another man? Glory also (saith he) as I understand, is spread more largely. For it requireth the consent of many men.

and:

> "The opinion of one man (saith he) sufficeth not to give glory and renowne vnto another."

and—the Latin being simply "laus nihil aliud quam vox est, vox autem bonum non est":

> But praise (saith he) is but a voice spread in the ayre, and that a word meriteth not the name of good.[28]

Claritas, for which Lodge takes *gloria* as synonym (justifiably, I think, at this point in that word's long eventful history); *fama*; *laus*; *existimatio*; *opinio*; *vox*; glory; fame; report; praise; opinion; voice. Let us add *honor* and *nomen*, honour and name. These are the words Shakespeare inherited.

It is a set of words describing certain relationships between a man and other men, all seen as together forming a group or community; relationships that will or may survive the death of that individual man, on the unvoiced assumption that the community will have a continuing existence.

Gloria is an intensification of honour; it is the relationships described by honour that come first. The most famous definition of *honor* is certainly Cicero's: "cum honos sit præmium virtutis iudicio studioque civium delatum ad aliquem, qui eum sententiis, qui suffragiis adeptus est, is mihi et honestus et honoratus videtur." [29] Here, in the opening clause, Cicero is, in fact, translating a phrase from Aristotle, in the *Nicomachean Ethics*. And these passages of Aristotle, with Cicero himself, and some passages from Stoic writers were to be be the main sources for sixteenth-century discussion. Aristotle is concerned to show that τιμή—honour—is not the "good". It is the end of the political or public life, but it cannot be the final good because it is extrinsic to the subject: it is thought to depend on those who confer honour rather than on him who receives it.[30]

Later, we have honour—"the due of the gods and what is desired by the eminent and awarded as the meed of victory in the most glorious contests"—as "the greatest of external goods".[31] And in the *Rhetoric* he lists the marks of honour—a list that was to be repeated, brought up to date, commented on—in many a sixteenth-century discourse:

> sacrifices; commemoration, in verse or prose; privileges; grants of land; precedence; sepulchres; statues; pensions; among foreigners, obeisances and giving place; and such gifts as are among various bodies of men regarded as marks of honour.[32]

The marks of honour demonstrate the relationship an individual has with his community, and with the continuing city; but they follow a judgment made on him, a judgment of value. Honouring is an act of which he is the subject, proceeding from *existimatio*, estimation, issuing in *laus*.

Who judges and who praises? Ideally the whole community. This, we are told, was fundamental to the prime meaning of the Roman *gloria*. Even to ask the question was to question and modify the whole concept of *gloria* as stimulus and reward of action; and this happened, we are told, in the last century of the Republic, under the pressure of social and political changes, and found its formulations in the disquiet of Greek philosophers. The disquiet was about the basis of the judgment that issues in the marks of honour; and is focused on the word δόξα with its double sense of my opinion, *opinio*, and the opinion others have of me. What certainty does *opinio* hold? If it holds none, what then is the basis of fame, reputation, renown, which *is* opinion?—a question Cicero and Seneca received from the Stoics. A temporary way of answering it is to restrict the judgment and the verdict to those competent to make it: *bonorum virorum secunda opinio*.[33] With *gloria* or *honor* goes *fama*:

> Gloria est frequens de aliquo fama cum laude.[34]

Gloria and *honor* depend on *fama*, and *fama* comes from *opinio*. *Fama*, my fame, is what people say about me: it is the utterance of the judgment or opinion. One citizen says to another in the first scene of *Coriolanus*:

> Consider you what services he has done for his country [35]

and gets the answer

> Very well, and could be content to give him good report for't but that he pays himself with being proud.[36]

This good report is quite strictly the *fama* which is *praemium* for Coriolanus' services. But from the beginning *Fama's* words are dangerously ambiguous; for *Fama* contains *Rumor*:

> famam atque rumores pars altera consensum civitatis et velut publicum testimonium vocat: altera sermonem sine ullo certo auctore dispersum, cui malignitas initium dederit, incrementum credulitas.[37]

And it is of *Fama-Rumor* that Virgil and Ovid made their powerful and fortunate images. Ovid's House of Fame, you remember, is made of sounding brass:

> tota fremit vocesque refert iteratque quod audit;
> nulla quies intus nullaque silentia parte ...
> atria turba tenet: veniunt, leve vulgus, euntque
> mixtaque cum veris passim commenta vagantur
> milia rumorum confusaque verba volutant;
> e quibus hi vacuas inplent sermonibus aures. . . .[38]

Fame's connections with words, breath, air, wind, are established in the classical images. Her trumpet figures this connection. The first instance I have found of the metaphor is in Juvenal,[39] and the full development seems to be certainly post-classical, but Fama was *nuntia veri* in Virgil,[40] and very often indeed, in other writers, *nuntia*. And there are the potent Virgilian phrases: the *ventosa gloria* [41] of which the unlucky warrior speaks to Camilla, and the splendid line in his own prayer to the Muses:

> et meministis enim, divæ, et memorare potestis;
> ad nos vix tenuis famae perlabitur aura.[42]

Shakespeare knows the tradition. We hear in *Romeo and Juliet* of "Three civil brawls bred of an airy word" [43]; in *Troilus and Cressida* of "that breath fame blows" and of fame's trump and "Having his ear full of his airy fame".[44] But the whole image had been shown in *Henry IV*, Part II, where, as Induction, Rumour enters "painted full of tongues", making the wind her post-horse. The trumpet is no longer an attribute of *Fama-Rumor*: it *is Fama-Rumor*, and included in the metaphor is the mob:

> Rumour is a pipe
> Blown by surmises, jealousies, conjectures,
> And of so easy and so plain a stop
> That the blunt monster with uncounted heads,
> The still discordant wav'ring multitude,
> Can play upon it. . . . [45]

This is Ovid's mob. Or Cicero's, when in his Stoic vein, he rejects popular judgment: fame, he says—*famam popularem*—cannot be counted a good when it is called into being by the united judgment of fools and knaves (*stultorum inproborumque*) and if things like fine eyes or a good colour are to be so considered then the philosopher's seriousness is no better than the *vulgi opinione stultorumque turba*.[46] Or Montaigne's in his essay on Glory, when he rejects "honor and glory, which is nought but a favourable judgement that is made of us". "And the judgement of our inclinations and actions (the waightiest and hardest matter that is) we referre it to the idle breath of the vaine voice of the common sort and base raskalitie. . . . In this breathie confusion of bruites, and frothy Chaos of reports and of vulgar opinions, which still push us on, no good course can be established." [47] For honour, glory, and fame are not to be dissociated. They are all favourable judgments, and the expression of the judgment is in speech, words, voices, which are breath and air, or wind, because the voice that utters does so through the vehicles of breath and air. It is because of this complex that I have tried to describe that Falstaff can be made to say

"What is honour? A word. What is in that word? Honour. What is that honour? Air."[48]

IV

Honour, Name and Fame are words, *voces*. They are voices because voice is both uttering and what is uttered; they are acts of judgment or opinion issuing in words. Their relationship to their subject is that of word to things. A word has two relationships: to him who utters it, and to its subject. Further, uttering happens in a community and establishes a relationship between the subject and that community; words are what the community says about him. They must be right, and the rightness of the relationship lies in its truth. It must be true between speaker and word, and true between word and thing. Language, what people say to each other about things, is constitutive of society, of the civil life. Working within the scheme I have outlined, exploiting and realizing its semantic possibilities as only Shakespeare in his full greatness could, Shakespeare offers a show of the civil life in terms of empty, perverted, destructive relationships between speaker and utterance, word and subject, which is between man and man and man and himself. In this play no one is innocent, except Virgilia who is silent: "My gracious silence." [49]

Honour and fame are words that go with the deed. The formal position —shown in the honouring of Coriolanus in the field—is simple. It posits a simple direct act, involving recognition, between word and deed. Honour is naming the deed. They cannot be separated. In the city honour is not given, the deed is not named without request—"policy", which expresses the way of keeping society together, imposes this. The act of naming is expressed by voices.

Of all formulas connected with the word none is more ancient than that which, in various versions, states an opposition between word and deed. This formula is basic for the play. Deeds, blows, acts are consistently opposed to words—in simple ways like this:

Has struck more blows for Rome
Than thou hast spoken words [50]

or:

When blows have made me stay, I fled from words.[51]

But the formula mutates into an opposition between deed, and word as *vox*; voice. It is the implied ground of that speech I have already quoted:

Here come moe voices.
Your voices. For your voices I have fought;
Watch'd for your voices; for your voices bear
Of wounds two dozen odd. . . . [52]

Voices, *voces* are the opposite of deeds or acts. They are devalued further through their definition as breath, light and empty; and stinking breath, offensive. Yet the mob's voices are intolerable because they are voices that are acts: acts of uttering that are acts of decision. Voice is deed and not deed in the same moment. Coriolanus' deeds, which must be named, fall into this nexus, the relationship between name and thing is disrupted: deed must be *honour*, its name, its *voice*. Deed, being named, passes into its opposite: voice.

In seeking the voices Coriolanus is a subject looking for his name: it is his name that will be uttered. But the search leads him into the gravest danger. He must ask.

"The price is to ask it kindly", says a citizen.[53] In Coriolanus' mind to ask is to beg. He sees himself as a beggar troubling the poor with begging, the napless vesture of humility as a disguise. When he takes it off, he says, he will know himself again.

> ... It is a part
> That I shall blush in acting.[54]

The beggar is like the actor: he mimics what he is not and utters words that are not his. The danger for Coriolanus is that to get his voice he must seem what he is not and utter words that are false and have no right relationship to the speaker: analogous relationships of falsity. Still more is required of him: the trap springs a second time. Acting and speech again go together. Brought in to persuade her son that he must formally appear before the Tribunes and the people, answer the charges brought against him and accept their verdict, their voice, for otherwise the city will be destroyed, Volumnia instructs Coriolanus that he must act a part and speak the words appropriate to his role of suppliant for mercy, and she seeks to convince him that to do so is consistent with his "honour". Coriolanus opposes to all this the idea of nature, disposition, truth, himself. Words and action must correspond directly to the nature which is a man's truth. This idea of his about words is reiterated through the play. It is recognized by friends and enemies alike:

> His heart's his mouth;
> What his breast forges, that his tongue must vent.[55]

Volumnia allows for it; he must speak to the people not

> ... by th' matter which your heart prompts you,
> But with such words that are but roted in
> Your tongue, though but bastards and syllables
> Of no allowance to your bosom's truth.[56]

Coriolanus is persuaded. Then he is permitted a moment of illumination— he cannot stand by it because his mother, not arguing, but taunting, dominates him—when he knows that to accept the role will be to destroy himself:

> ... I will not do't.
> Lest I surcease to honour mine own truth
> And by my body's action teach my mind
> A most inherent baseness.[57]

There is, he says, a truth; it must be named in honour by himself and no other. Honour is the name for it and he must give it. To do otherwise, to utter words that do not correspond or perform actions that contradict, is to alter his very being.

The relationship is between "I" and "myself". To trace the history that made possible this great leap, through Stoic and Christian—Montaigne in such a context quotes St. Paul: *Gloria nostra est testimonium conscientiæ nostræ*, and Montaigne in his quotation is following Augustine,[58] and through the critique of chivalry with which Shakespeare is explicitly and persistently concerned: the history of the interiorizing of honour, which is never quite complete—all this would be beyond my power. Shakespeare is using at this moment the language of the Schools. It is the only time in his whole *oeuvre* that he uses the word inherent; and I cannot believe that he did not fully know its technical use in connection with substance. What Coriolanus is being asked to do is to transform disgracefully his being.

In *Troilus and Cressida*, where honour and love are treated, conceptually, as cases of "estimation", and the question is specifically asked whether value is intrinsic or extrinsic, the doubleness of Cressida—Troilus's Cressida, Diomede's Cressida, every man's Cressida—becomes, with painful irony—for it was Troilus who had insisted that value lies only in estimation—proof that a thing can be itself and other than itself in the same moment; and this denies the principle of oneness, which guarantees being, which rests on the sacred and indivisible *unitas*:

> If there be rule in Unitie itself
> This is not she [59]—

he cries. Being is disrupted and the fabric of the Universe torn.

In *Coriolanus* we are concerned only with the community or city, *civitas*, localized as Rome, the *urbs*, in danger of destruction. Questions of the self, its maintenance or destruction, rise within the social context and are limited to that. A name stands at the centre of the play; and it is in the name that these questions are focused.

The name is a voice, a word, one of the two fundamental parts of language, which the ancients distinguished, names or nouns and verbs. It is the vocable that belongs to a man:

> Nomen est quod uni cuique personae datur, quo suo quaeque proprio et certo vocabulo appellatur.[60]

It can go with Fame, in the Name and Fame formula, because a name is the word people use about me. It states both individuality and membership of family and group. It is the third name, the *cognomen*, Coriolanus, that most strictly marks the individual: no-one else has this:

> The third, was some addition geven, either for some acte or notable service, or for some marke on their face, or of some shape of their bodie, or els for some speciall vertue they had.[61]

Giving the name "Coriolanus" to him is to give him fame, a name that will last, honour, a new individuality, like a baptism:

> By deed-achieving honour newly nam'd.[62]

It asserts his uniqueness, but a uniqueness that is an *assertion*, a uniqueness given in relationship to those who gave it. When he comes to Aufidius, muffled, disguised, and the question "What is your name" echoes, he answers, as we saw: "*Only that name remains.*" [63] All else is devoured. Cominius, on a fruitless embassy from Rome, later, reports

> ... 'Coriolanus'
> He would not answer to; forbad all names;
> He was a kind of nothing, titleless
> Till he had forg'd himself a name i' th' fire
> Of burning Rome.[64]

In the scene that immediately follows, when Menenius goes to see Coriolanus, the theme is pointed, serio-comically, in his dialogue with the guards. He appears as Coriolanus' reporter: he is in estimation with him: he is Coriolanus' liar—so the forthright soldiers turn the phrase:

> The virtue of your name
> Is not here passable [65]

they greet him with; and mockingly when he goes,

> *1 Watch.*   Now, sir, is your name Menenius?
> *2 Watch.*   'Tis a spell, you see, of much power! [66]

What is the relationship that word or name holds with the thing named? Here we come to the old story of whether words or names relate to their objects by nature or convention. Shakespeare knew both accounts. His statement of one has become proverbial:

> 'Tis but thy name that is my enemy;
> Thou art thyself, though not a Montague.
> What's Montague? It is nor hand, nor foot.
> Nor arm, nor face, nor any other part
> Belonging to a man. O be some other name!
> What's in a name? That which we call a rose
> By any other name would smell as sweet;
> So Romeo would, were he not Romeo call'd,
> Retain that dear perfection which he owes
> Without that title. Romeo, doff thy name,
> And for thy name, which is no part of thee,
> Take all myself.[67]

It is a virtuoso handling of the argument. Put it beside the paragraph which introduces Montaigne's essay on *Glory* (he is working from Sebond):

> There is both name, and the thing: the name, is a voice which noteth, and
> signifieth the thing: the name is neither part of thing nor of substance: it is a
> stranger-piece joyned to the thing, and from it.[68]

But when Adam named the beasts he named them according to their natures: the connection was real not conventional. Further, as Dr. Walker has said, in his discussion of this view in the sixteenth-century Neo-Platonic texts: "the word is not merely like a quality of the thing it designates . . . it is, or exactly represents, its essence or substance." [69] So it came about that the name has power, is magical; and so it can be said

that the name Menenius carried to Coriolanus has virtue, is *a spell of power*.
And on this view Juliet is wrong—and the play shows it—when she
argues that Romeo's self can be dissevered from his name, which is indeed
a part of him. Shakespeare does not always laugh, like the sceptical
soldiers. It seems to me that the name, in his usages, hovers in an ambiguous zone, its status not quite determined, and the possibilities capable
of powerful exploitation. Take that sinister little scene in *Julius Cæsar*
when the mob, loosed by Antony, blind and frantic, encounters the poet
Cinna. The answer to his scream

> I am not Cinna the conspirator.

is

> It is no matter, his name's Cinna; pluck but his name out of his heart . . .[70]

It is precisely the ambiguity that makes that so resonant. And it is, for
instance, in such ambiguity, such doubt, that lie the tragedy and destruction of Richard II, who has to learn to ask what is the connection between
his name and him.

> Is not the king's name twenty thousand names?
> Arm, arm my name! a puny subject strikes
> At thy great glory.[71]

In the abdication scene meditations on crown and self—"I must nothing
be"—are followed by refusal of forms of address:

> . . . I have no name, no title—
> No, not that name was given me at the font—
> But 'tis usurped. . . . [72]

and the call for a mirror. Name and mirror: guarantees of a continuing
self. Meditations on either are dangerous, and subversive. And, at the end,
in prison, Richard's recreation of himself through a sequence of images
comes back to this:

> . . . Then am I king'd again; and by and by
> Think that I am unking'd by Bolingbroke,
> And straight am nothing. . . .[73]

Montaigne, whose essay so clearly demonstrates that the argument
about Fame is an argument about Name, when he rejects honour, glory,
fame, rejects his name. His surname is common to all his race; his
Christian name belongs to anyone that wants it: "I have no name that is
sufficiently mine." "As for me", he says, "I hold that I am but in my selfe;
and of this other life of mine, which consisteth in the knowledge of my
friends, being simply and barely considered in my selfe, well I wot, I
neither feel fruite or jovissance of it, but by the vanity of fantasticall
opinion." [74]

This way is not permitted to Coriolanus, for he is involved in the active
life. He has a name that is sufficiently his, unique. Banished from Rome,
it is all that remains to him. And this he rejects, as he has rejected the city:

"I banish you." [75] Properly—the City gave it. He must forge a new name in the fires of Rome, as Herostratus—it is the example always used— perpetuated his name by burning down the great temple of Diana at Ephesus.[76] Without "Coriolanus" he is "a kind of nothing, titleless".[77] What is nameless is monstrous, "a deed without a name". It belongs to the realm that is not subjugated. "When he shall be able to call the creatures by their true names he shall again command them", wrote Bacon from his dream of knowledge that is power.[78] Naming gives identity to nothings. It is also the poet's function: his pen gives shapes to the forms of things unknown, products of the imagination,

> "to airy nothing a local habitation and a name . . ."

Shakespeare is here using as a frame of reference a great argument of which he shows elsewhere—as in *The Tempest*—full knowledge.

The monstrous, the unsubjugated, the unknown, the nothing, are what is outside the frontier of language, or the frontier of the human. For language is vehicle and expression of *ratio*, of reason, of what makes man man. A Macbeth denies his humanity, and an idiot's gabble is the metaphor for the final nonsense to which he has reduced his world. The origins of language, if we follow those ancient writers who denied that it was given by a God or some nameless lawmaker, are inextricably connected with the joining together of men in groups—"in conversation with each other", with the origins of building and law.[79] Naming is within the family and the community: it asserts individuality through relationships. The community, the rational, human life, is defined by the walls of the city: it is the life of *conversazione civile*, civil intercourse, *civil conversation*—and our meaning for that word was separated out of the first. The bond is language. The city of *Coriolanus* is certainly London, but first it is Rome, *Urbs, the* city: consciousness of the city is sustained throughout the play, in awe, question or doubt: often from the lips of the unimportant, the bystanders. Banished from the city, banishing the city, Coriolanus leaves the pale of humanity: he sees himself and is seen as a lonely dragon, one of those fabled or perhaps real monsters from which men, in story, sheltered themselves behind the city walls. When Aufidius' servant says:

> "Where dwell'st thou?"

he answers

> "I' the city of kites and crows"[80]:

a total reversal of meaning—scavenger birds that feed on carcases.

And finally, he is titleless, a kind of nothing. To lose the *name* is to lose the self, and at that moment when the women come to intercede he asserts his singleness, his refusal of relationships: he will

> stand
> As if a man were author of himself
> And knew no other kin.[81]

He cannot sustain this, and breaks himself; and indeed in the Shakespearian world it is blasphemy. From the beginning Coriolanus had been accused of denying relationships in the city: of pride, of speaking of the people as though he were a God to punish "not a man of their infirmity".[82] The basis is in North where Shakespeare read that Coriolanus was "churlishe, uncivill and altogether unfit for any mans conversation". [83] Consistently he equates "good words" to the people as false words: "flattery".

Finally he accepts again his relationships, with mother, wife and child; with the city in which his son will perpetuate his name, of whose history his name will be part. This identification brings accusation in Corioli: his last outbursts are reassertions of his name, his Romanness, of himself, his Fame—they go together:

> If you have writ your annals true, 'tis there,
> That, like an eagle in a dove-cote I
> Fluttered your Volscians in Corioli.
> Alone I did it.[84]

This great play, relentless, unremitting, misunderstood, offers us no easy comfort of confirmed anticipation or imagined identification. And not the liberating ritual comfort of tragedy. It is a show of the civil life. The city must stand and must continue, for outside it there is the monstrous, or the nothing. But within the walls absolutes turn out to be instrumental; the words that identify and bind become words that debase and destroy: whoops, or hoots, curses, lies, flatteries, voices, stinking breath. Words are torn from what they signify. They pass into their antonyms. Deeds are not— deeds. Names are not—names. The absoluteness of the self, the I, cannot be maintained; but the necessary relationship of the I with name or fame destroys. In this city to speak is to be guilty.[85]

NOTES

1. The following is the text of a lecture delivered at the Warburg Institute of the University of London on 2 May 1962.
2. *Plutarch's Lives of the Noble Grecians and Romans, Englished by Sir Thomas North* ... with an introduction by G. Wyndham (Tudor Translations, London 1895), Vol. II, p. 144.
3. II. ii .81-83. References to Act, scene and line number are given as in William Shakespeare, *The Complete Works*, ed. P. Alexander (London, 1951).
4. I. ix. 58-66.
5. II. i. 153-7.
6. II. i. 163-5.
7. *Tusculan Disputations*, I. xiv. 31 (Loeb Classical Library, pp. 38-39).
8. V. iii. 126-7.
9. V. iii. 142-8.
10. IV. v. 52-64.
11. IV. v. 65-78.

12. North's Plutarch, *ed. cit.* Vol. II, p. 170.
13. *Hamlet*, v. ii. 347-8.
14. *E.g. Les Vies des hommes illustres, grecs et romains, comparées l'une avec l'autre, par Plutarque de Choeronée, translatées ... par Jaques Amyot ...* 2nd edn., printing of 1572, fol. 128^r, 130^r; North's Plutarch, *ed. cit.* Vol. II, pp. 158, 166-7.
15. *Ed. cit.* fol. 130^r.
16. *Ed. cit.* Vol. II, p. 166.
17. J. E. Neale, *The Elizabethan House of Commons* (London, 1949), Chaps. 3-6, esp. pp. 87 ff. The quotation is from p. 88.
18. III. iii. 8-10.
19. Neale, *op. cit.* p. 87.
20. II. iii. 122-8.
21. III. iii. 122-3.
22. IV. vi. 147-8.
23. IV. vi. 97-9.
24. *Richard II*, III. ii. 54-57.
25. II. ii. 147-8.
26. II. i. 225-6.
27. *Epistulae morales*, CII (Loeb Classical Library, Vol. III, pp. 172-7).
28. *The Workes of Lucius Annaeus Seneca, newly inlarged and corrected by Thomas Lodge* (London, 1614), p. 428.
29. *Brutus*, 281 (Loeb Classical Library, pp. 242-3).
30. *Nicomachean Ethics*, 1095b (Loeb Classical Library, pp. 14-15).
31. *Ibid.* 1123a (Loeb Classical Library, pp. 214-15).
32. *Rhetoric*, 1361a (Loeb Classical Library, pp. 52-53).
33. Seneca, *loc. cit.*
34. Cicero, *De inventione* II. 166 (Loeb Classical Library, pp. 332-3).
35. I. i. 28-29.
36. I i. 30-32.
37. Quintilian, *Institutio oratoria*, v. iii. 1 (Loeb Classical Library, Vol. II, pp. 162-3).
38. *Metamorphoses*, XII. 47 ff. (Loeb Classical Library, Vol. II, pp. 184-5).
39. Juvenal, VII. 71 (Loeb Classical Library, pp. 142-3).
40. *Aeneid*, IV. 188 (Loeb Classical Library, Vol. I, pp. 408-9).
41. *Aeneid*, XI. 708 (Loeb Classical Library, Vol. II, pp. 282-3).
42. *Aeneid*, VII. 645-6 (Loeb Classical Library, Vol. II, pp. 46-47).
43. *Romeo and Juliet*, I. i. 87.
44. *Troilus and Cressida*, I. iii. 244; III. iii. 210; I. iii. 144.
45. II *Henry IV*, Ind. 15-20.
46. *Tusculan Disputations*, V. 46 (Loeb Classical Library, pp. 472-3).
47. *Of Glory*, in *The Essaies ... done into English by John Florio ...* with an introduction by G. Saintsbury (Tudor Translations, London, 1893), Book II, Chap. 16, Vol. II, pp. 354-5.
48. I *Henry IV*, v. i. 130-2.
49. II. i. 166.
50. IV. ii. 19-20.
51. II. ii. 70.
52. II. iii. 122-5.
53. II. iii. 73.
54. II. ii. 142-3.
55. III. i. 257-8.
56. III. ii. 54-57.
57. III. ii. 120-3.
58. *Of Glory, ed. cit.* Vol. II, p. 353. The quotation from St. Paul is 2 Cor. i. 12. Cf. St. Augustine, *Hom.* xxxv (*Patrologia Latina*, xxxviii, col. 213 f.).

59. *Troilus and Cressida*, v. ii. 139-40.
60. Cicero, *De inventione*, I. 34 (Loeb Classical Library, pp. 70-71).
61. North's Plutarch, *ed. cit.* Vol. II, pp. 154-5.
62. II. i. 164.
63. iv. v. 73.
64. v. i. 11-15.
65. v. ii. 12-13.
66. v. ii. 91-92.
67. *Romeo and Juliet*, II. ii. 38-49.
68. *Of Glory, ed. cit.* Vol. II, p. 348.
69. D. P. Walker, *Spiritual and Demonic Magic from Ficino to Campanella*, (Studies of the Warburg Institute, XXII, London, 1958), pp. 80-81.
70. *Julius Caesar*, III. iii. 32-34.
71. *Richard II*, III. ii. 85-87.
72. *Richard II*, IV. i. 255-7.
73. *Richard II*, v. v. 36-38.
74. *Of Glory, ed. cit.* Vol. II, p. 358.
75. III. iii. 125.
76. Cf. e.g. Montaigne, *Of Glory, ed. cit.* Vol. II, p. 357.
77. v. i. 13.
78. *Of the Interpretation of Nature*, I (*Works*, eds. Ellis and Spedding, Vol. III, London, 1859, p. 222).
79. Lucretius, *De rerum natura*, V. 1011 ff. (Loeb Classical Library, pp. 412-15); Vitruvius, *De architectura*, II. 1 (Loeb Classical Library, Vol. I, pp. 76-79); cf. Cicero, *De inventione* I. 2-3 (Loeb Classical Library, pp. 4-7). For other ancient accounts see Lucretius, *De rerum natura*, ed. C. Bailey, Oxford, 1947, Vol. III (Commentary), pp. 1487 ff.
80. IV. v. 37, 42.
81. v. iii. 35-37.
82. III. i. 80-81.
83. North's Plutarch, *ed. cit.* Vol. II, p. 144.
84. v. vi. 114-17.
85. The basis of my work has been the great dictionaries, concordances, and indexes, especially the articles *fama* and *gloria* in the *Thesaurus linguae latinae*. I have also found the following studies important: U. Knoche, 'Der romische Ruhmesgedanke', *Philologus* LXXXIX (NF XLIII), 1934, pp. 102-24; A. D. Leeman, *Gloria. Cicero's waardering van de roem en haar achtergrond* ... (with English summary) (Rotterdam, 1949); A. J. Vermeulen, *The semantic Development of Gloria in early-Christian Latin* (Nijmegen, 1956); C. Mohrmann, 'Note sur Doxa' in her *Études sur le Latin des Chrétiens* (Rome, 1958); J. Daniélou, *Théologie du Judéo-Christianisme* (Paris, 1958); C. Bailey, Commentary on Lucretius *De natura rerum*, cited in note 79 above; Arnold Williams, *The Common Expositor: An account of the Commentaries on Genesis 1527-1633* (Chapel Hill, 1948); P. Villey, *Les Sources et l'evolution des Essais de Montaigne* (Paris, 1933), Vol. I; P. Ure, 'A note on "Opinion" in Daniel, Greville and Chapman', *Modern Language Review*, Vol. XLVI (1951), pp. 331-8 (a particularly valuable study of the topic); P. Ure, ed., *King Richard II* (Arden edn.), 1956 etc.; V. B. Heltzel's edn. of Robert Ashley's *Of Honour* (San Marino, 1947), which has a very useful introduction and commentary. Curtis Brown Watson, *Shakespeare and the Renaissance Concept of Honor* (Princeton, 1960), I conceive to be mistaken in method and conclusions. I should like to thank my colleagues in the Department of Classics in the University of Reading for their readiness to answer questions, and Dr. Whitney Bolton and Mr. J. B. Trapp for help with the text.

T. E. Lawrenson

VOLTAIRE AND SHAKESPEARE

ORDEAL BY TRANSLATION

"Quand on cherche à traduire il faut choisir son auteur, comme on choisit un amy, d'un goût conforme au nôtre."
François-Marie Arouet, dit Voltaire.

"How absolute the knave is! we must speak by the card or equivocation will undo us." William Shakespeare.

In the twentieth century, no British student of French literature can spend a couple of decades in the company of Racinian tragedy without developing an enhanced appreciation of Shakespeare, and such a statement can be made without the slightest disparagement of the French dramatic poet. The claustrophobic intensity of Racine's tragic verse, authoritatively limited both in vocabulary and measure,[1] perfect expression of the tragic hero imprisoned in his condition, added to the apparent ease with which the author moves about in the rigidly circumscribed unities and *bienséances*, combine to convey an impression of intense cataclysm expressed in a highly organized manner. It is as though one were at the still eye of a cyclone. This is a form of aesthetic experience afforded by Racine, and by Racine alone. A considerable number of lesser poets were employing the same formula at the same time and failing, as Voltaire was to fail nearly a century later.

Now, whatever the aesthetic experiences afforded by Shakespearian tragedy, the reader may agree with me that they are not *that*; he will at the same time perhaps forgive a French scholar for not attempting to say just what they are, and for not, as the French would say, putting his hand into that particular *panier de crabes*.

The foregoing remarks constitute but the first of a series of banalities necessary to anyone who would re-open the topic of Voltaire and Shakespeare, so thoroughly worked over by Lounsbury and others.[2] However, though the complementary nature of Shakespeare and Racine may seem commonplace enough to us, it is none the less a recent banality which had hardly been mooted in France as late as 1823, when Stendhal published his *Racine et Shakespeare*, in which he gave his famous definition of Romanticism:

Le *romanticisme* est l'art de présenter aux peuples les œuvres littéraires qui, dans l'état actuel de leurs habitudes et de leurs croyances, sont susceptibles de leur donner le plus de plaisir possible.

Le *classicisme*, au contraire, leur présente la littérature qui donnait le plus grand plaisir possible à leurs arrière-grands-pères.

From which we are to infer that although Stendhal will concede that Racine in his own day may have corresponded to the definition of a Romantic, he is now, in 1823, a poet who has nothing to say to the condition of contemporary society. The type of drama that does say something is that of Shakespeare. The two poets are thus still mutually exclusive, since one is bidden to choose between them.

This is just what Voltaire exhorted the whole of Europe to do, and with a vehemence which increased with age. The history of this process has, it must be repeated, been so well chronicled by Lounsbury that only the immense and comforting plea of a Shakespearian quatercentenary, together with the desire to look a little more closely at what the eighteenth-century public was given (in French) as Shakespeare, may be said to excuse this essay.

Voltaire repeatedly averred that he was the first to introduce the knowledge of Shakespeare to Europe. This is widely accepted, and rightly so, as a general truth, in the sense that he was the first to whom the whole of continental Europe listened, and the paucity of other popularizers before his *Lettres Philosophiques* of 1734 (in their French version) is adduced as evidence.[3] His French predecessors in this matter are not however altogether as undistinguished as has occasionally been implied, and it cannot be said that Shakespeare was unknown in France before Voltaire. Admittedly, it was hardly conceded in that country that England had any poets at all, much less poets in the English language. Jusserand, at the end of the last century, described the general consensus of French tourist opinion about the English: the women were pretty, the men boorish, and the food terrible.[4] The traffic between the two countries increased however after the Restoration, and two of the French travellers contrive to mention the poet in their accounts: Muralt (who prefers Ben Jonson), and Moreau de Brasey. According to the former, "England is a land of passions and catastrophes, so much so that Shakespeare, one of the best of their poets of the past, has put a good deal of their history into tragedies". The latter says that "a certain Shakespeare" has left a masterly foundation for the English theatre in his excellent plays, and then adds that this taste has been perfected in Mr. Addison's *Cato*, a position which we shall see Voltaire adopting later. The knowledge of the English theatre makes some headway thereafter, even Jeremy Collier's outburst being translated in 1715. Translation of dramatic texts themselves remains however extremely rare in the seventeenth century. The English reputation among the French is that of thinkers, not dramatic poets (the English "pensent profondément" says La Fontaine), and Muralt's letters are not published till 1725, although written in 1694, while Moreau de

Brasey is not published until 1744. The earliest critical mention of Shakespeare given by Jusserand is the catalogue entry in the library of Louis XIV:

> Will. Shakespeare,
> Poeta anglicus,
> Opera poetica, continentia tragoedias, comoedias et historiolas.
> Angle, Lond. Th. Cotes, 1632, fo.

The librarian comments: "This English poet has a fairly fine (*belle*) imagination, he thinks naturally and expresses himself with delicacy: but these fine qualities are clouded over by the filth (*ordures*) that he puts into his comedies." Applied to the tragedies rather than the comedies, this was to be the French leitmotif for more than a century, intoned chiefly by Voltaire. There is a copy of the comedies in the library of Fouquet, and the poet is mentioned in 1685-86 by Baillet in his *Jugement des Savants*. Boyer mentions his name, linking it with that of Euripides, but obviously preferring Dryden. This virtually exhausts the seventeenth century. In the early part of the eighteenth the movement accelerates somewhat, and in 1717 de la Roche opens a review in French (published from Amsterdam) devoted specifically to English letters. The *Journal Littéraire* of the Hague publishes also in 1717 a "dissertation sur la poésie anglaise": Hamlet, it says, is a mixture of "strong and energetic speeches" and "lowness" (*traits rampants*); Shakespeare is held by the English in exorbitant esteem: "an unruly genius, who imitated nobody, but, drawing everything from his own imagination, has, as it were, abandoned his works to the care of Fortune, without choosing the necessary and noble circumstances of his subjects and without discarding those which are useless or unseemly. One cannot see, in his plays, that by his own reasoning he has deduced, from the nature of tragedy, the least fixed rule to replace those of the ancients which he had neglected to study."[5]

This criticism sets the tone for that of eighteenth-century France, and it was to be Voltaire's tone. What differs essentially as between one criticism and another is the weight to be attached to the "beauties" and the "lowness" to be discerned in the author. The abbé Prévost enthuses, more than most, about the English drama, including a mention of *Hamlet* in the general anglophilia, but feels equally obliged to enter the by now almost customary reservation: some of the tragedies are disfigured by a mixture of buffooneries unworthy of the buskined muse. The *Mémoires d'un homme de qualité*, from which the above is culled, appeared from 1728 to 1731, and bring us in time to Voltaire's first mention of Shakespeare. Much of what he was to say had, then, been already said, though tersely and sporadically.

Voltaire was to say it better, more vociferously, and in greater detail. He was also to say it for over half a century; and, final distinction, he was to be listened to.

The letter to Bolingbroke which forms the dedication of Voltaire's *Discourse on Tragedy* compares the stages of England and France. As

Lounsbury properly points out Voltaire, writing to a man who shared his opinions on regularity in tragedy, felt that he did not have to "combat any undue and unjustifiable admiration".[6] The result is, at the outset of what we might call the writer's "Shakespearian" career, kindness towards, and appreciation of, the poet such as he was not to enjoy again, for it is generally agreed that Voltaire became more savage to Shakespeare as time went on.[7] We see also another, and complementary, fact. Voltaire is not only at his kindest, but when, in the course of his letter to Bolingbroke he essays a translation from *Julius Caesar*, again in the opinion of Lounsbury "It is both the earliest and the most faithful of any attempt on his part to reproduce a passage of Shakespeare".

It is possible to attribute this to the freshness of Voltaire's knowledge of English: that he studied the language assiduously has been amply demonstrated,[8] and he himself speaks in the same letter of his two year's study of the language, and of how he was practically thinking in English, and experiencing difficulty in writing in French. But another possibility springs to the mind: Voltaire is making an attempt to render Shakespeare effectively at this stage because the translation itself is to serve no polemical, anti-Shakespearian purpose. For the moment, as he returns to writing in French, there seems to be a real nostalgia for the liberty of blank verse: "What frightened me most in returning to this occupation was the severity of our poetry, and the slavery of rhyme."[9] He regrets too the great facility of *enjambement* in blank verse, and the English ability to create, where necessary, new terms "which are always adopted by you when they are sonorous, intelligible and necessary". The Frenchman, he opines, a slave to rhyme, is frequently obliged to use four lines to express a thought that the Englishman can render in one. The English poet says what he wants, the French only what he can.

On the topic of rhyme he is adamant. It is essential to French tragedy, where the verse form permits few *enjambements*, where the long and short measure of the syllables is insufficient to produce a harmonious effect by itself, and where left to themselves, without rhyme, neither caesura nor a given number of feet would be adequate to distinguish French verse from French prose. Whether this is true or not, it is Voltaire nailing his colours to the mast, and this opinion must of necessity condition the type of translation into French that he will make of a given author: or at least we might think so.

Thus armed, he proceeds to a consideration of Shakespeare's *Julius Caesar*. Repeating his theme of barbarous irregularities rubbing shoulders with sublime beauties, he instances as an example of the latter Brutus' address to the Romans in Act III, scene ii. The English prose is done into French prose, and despite Voltaire's strictures on prose tragedy, the French is none the worse for being prose. The speech in the original has received a rough handling from the earlier English critics, and this might be held to lend colour to Singer's strictures: "It is worthy of remark that Voltaire, who has stolen and transplanted into his tragedy of Brutus the fine speech

5*

of Antony to the people . . . affects to extol this address by Brutus, while he is most disingenuously silent on that of Antony, which he chose to purloin."[10] The fact remains that the translation is not without merit. The short-sentenced, ruthless chop-logic of which Voltaire was capable in French marries naturally (though there are reservations) the rugged attempt at unemotional logic in the English Brutus:

> Be patient till the last. Romans, countrymen, and lovers! hear me for my   1
> cause; and be silent, that you may hear: believe me for mine honour, and
> have respect to mine honour, that you may believe: censure me in your
> wisdom, and awake your senses, that you may the better judge. If there be
> any in this assembly, any dear friend of Caesar's, to him I say that Brutus'   5
> love to Caesar was no less than his. If then that friend demand why Brutus
> rose against Caesar, this is my answer: Not that I loved Caesar less, but that
> I loved Rome more. Had you rather Caesar were living, and die all slaves,
> than that Caesar were dead, to live all free men? As Caesar loved me, I
> weep for him; as he was fortunate, I rejoice at it; as he was valiant, I honour 10
> him; but, as he was ambitious, I slew him. There is tears for his love; joy for
> his fortune; honour for his valour; and death for his ambition. Who is here
> so base that he would be a bondman? If any, speak; for him have I offended.
> Who is here so vile that will not love his country? If any, speak; for him
> have I offended. I pause for a reply.   15
> *All:* None, Brutus, none.
> Then none have I offended. I have done no more to Caesar, than you shall
> do to Brutus. The question of his death is enrolled in the Capitol; his glory
> not extenuated, wherein he was worthy, nor his offences enforced, for which
> he suffered death.   20
> *Enter Antony and others, with Caesar's dead body.*
> Here comes his body, mourned by Mark Antony: who, though he had no
> hand in his death, shall receive the benefit of his dying, a place in the
> commonwealth; as which of you shall not? With this I depart: that, as I
> slew my best lover for the good of Rome, I have the same dagger for myself, 25
> when it shall please my country to need my death.
> *All:* Live, Brutus! live! live!

Voltaire's version is as follows:

> Romains, compatriotes, amis, s'il est quelqu'un de vous qui ait été attaché   1
> à César, qu'il sache que Brutus ne l'était pas moins : oui, je l'aimais, Romains;
> et si vous me demandez puorquoi j'ai versé son sang, c'est que j'aimais
> Rome davantage. Voudriez-vous voir César vivant, et mourir ses esclaves,
> plutôt que d'acheter votre liberté par sa mort? César était mon ami, je le   5
> pleure; il était heureux, j'applaudis à ses triomphes; il était vaillant, je
> l'honore: mais il était ambitieux, je l'ai tué. Y a-t-il quelqu'un parmi vous
> assez lâche pour regretter la servitude? S'il en est un seul, qu'il parle, qu'il
> se montre; c'est lui que j'ai offensé; y a-t-il quelqu'un assez infâme pour
> oublier qu'il est Romain? Qu'il parle; C'est lui seul qui est mon ennemi.   10
>
> *Chœur des Romains*
> Personne, non, Brutus, personne.
>
> *Brutus*
> Ainsi donc je n'ai offensé personne. Voici le corps du dictateur qu'on vous
> apporte; les derniers devoirs lui seront rendus par Antoine, par cet Antoine
> qui n'ayant point eu de part au châtiment de César, en retirera le même

avantage que moi; et que chacun de vous sente le bonheur inestimable 15
d'être libre! Je n'ai plus qu'un mot à vous dire: j'ai tué de cette main mon
meilleur ami pour le salut de Rome; je garde ce même poignard pour moi,
quand Rome me demandera ma vie.

Le Chœur

Vivez, Brutus, vivez à jamais!

In line 1 of the English version Voltaire prop :rly renders *lover* by *ami*
but this confronts him with the problem of avoiding excessive repetition
of that word, since Shakespeare uses *friend* three times and *lover* twice in
the passage. Thus, on the first occasion that *friend* is used (line 5) he
paraphrases accurately as "qui ait été attaché à", and this permits him to
avoid a direct (substantival) translation of *love* in line 6. The next use
of *friend* (line 6) is avoided less felicitously by "et si vous me demandez".
"Not that I loved Caesar less" is suppressed, possibly to avoid yet another
use of the *aimer-ami* group of words, and the antithetical, persuasive effect
of the phrase "I loved Rome more" is not thus apparent in "j'aimais Rome
davantage". Honest though the translator's purpose may be here, it
prompts the thought that the act of translation itself is an implied and
inescapable act of criticism of the original. The similar force of the juxtaposition of "living . . . die" in line 8 and "dead . . . live" in line 9 is
equally thrown away in the phrase "acheter votre liberté par sa mort",
which of course avoids a second use of the verb *vivre*. In the process, the
French Brutus is ceasing to become the naive logician that Shakespeare
made of him, and is turning into a somewhat polished orator. The
situation is restored a little by the nearly literal translation of the passage
"As Caesar loved me . . . I slew him". (Since Voltaire uses the rather
vague *heureux* for *fortunate*, he properly expands the meaning in the other
half of the phrase by translating "I rejoice at it" as "j'applaudis à ses
triomphes".) The second half of line 11, and line 12 continue to fill in the
picture of Brutus as drawn by the English poet, and as noticed by so many
commentators: "artificial jingle of short sentences" (Stevens), "Brutus will
present calmly and dispassionately the reasons for our Caesar's death"
(Knight), "curt sententious oratory" (Lloyd), "its studied primness and
epigrammatic finish contrast most unfavourably with the frank-hearted
yet artful eloquence of Antony" (Dowden). Lines 11 and 12 are vital in the
building up of these impressions, which could have been well transposed
into the French style of Voltaire. Yet he does not translate them at all. The
statutory avoidance of repetition ensures that the translator will fail to
capture the insistence of the two concealed blank verse lines "If any, speak,
for him have I offended" in his rendering of lines 12, 13, and 14-15, but he
makes assurance doubly sure by adding a supererogatory "qu'il se montre"
after the first "qu'il parle", which phrase is the only repetition he allows,
the second "him have I offended" becoming "c'est lui seul qui est mon
ennemi". "I pause for a reply" he does not deign to translate at all.
Similarly, the whole of lines 17, 18, 19, and 20 (with the exception of the
initial "Then none have I offended") remain untranslated, and collating

Voltaire and Shakespeare we suddenly stumble over the corpse of Caesar: it jumps its cue, so to speak. The remainder of the translation seems relatively unexceptionable, though the old libertarian Adam in the French sage causes him to give "le corps du dictateur" for "his body", and he shuns a direct translation of *commonwealth* (would not *chose publique*, i.e. *res publica*, have done well?) so that "et que chacun de vous sente le bonheur inestimable d'être libre" rejoins Voltaire's preoccupation with liberty and drifts away from the English "as which of you shall not".

The considerable omissions are intriguing. There is no special reason for thinking that he was not working from the full text, though there is the faint possibility that he was using transcriptions of his own in which he might have omitted passages that did not interest him.[11] The only lacuna not yet mentioned is in lines 1-4, with the exception of "Romans, countrymen and lovers". One can only surmise as to the reasons for these gaps, but in this latter case it is yet again worthy of note that the major translation difficulty stems from the fact that the words *hear, honour,* and *believe,* are each repeated. The repetition, translated, would have shocked the eighteenth-century French reader. The fact that these lines are intended to quell a turbulent crowd before Brutus enters into the real substance of his argument would not weigh heavily upon Voltaire, partly because that particular type of stage forethought was in any case foreign to the craft of the French tragic poem, and partly perhaps because Voltaire disapproved of the presence of this particular crowd on this particular stage: it was an impropriety within the terms of the "rules". The omission of "I have done no more to Caesar . . . for which he suffered death" is even more difficult to explain. It is possible that Stevens was right, and that Voltaire, having "borrowed" the more impressive speech of Mark Antony for his *Brutus,* did not quite feel the enthusiasm for the present one that he affected in his letter to Bolingbroke, and that consequently he was not inclined to bother overmuch with passages which are not immediately clear: "the question of his death is enrolled in the Capitol" (i.e. "the reason for his death has been duly minuted in the Senate") might have caused him difficulty and he could well have regarded it as obscure and therefore beneath his attention: all linguists do the same thing from time to time, and after all it is but a little step from the thought "ce qui n'est pas clair n'est pas français" to the exculpation "ce qui ne m'est pas clair à moi, je n'ai pas besoin de le traduire".

Be this as it may, the above represents Voltaire's most faithful attempt to reproduce a passage from Shakespeare, and we have seen what reservations are to be made. There is already a cavalier treatment of the text, and the act of translating itself implies a critical position.

When he returned from England to France, Voltaire brought out a French version of his *Essay on Epic Poetry,* and this time inserted a certain amount of matter concerning Shakespeare. He was still favourably inclined towards the poet. The English, he had discovered, were very impressed by their national bard: they called him the "divine" and (scandalously) preferred him to Addison's *Cato*.[12] The plays are described as "monstrosities", Voltaire brings exaggerated attention to bear, whether deliberately or no, on the "vulgarities" of sorcerers, peasants, buffoons, drunkards and grave-diggers, and yet, he finds, the whole is shot through with moments of sublimity. And these moments, he genuinely regrets, the French stage seems to be incapable of. Lounsbury is right here: these remarks are the apex of Voltaire's liberality about Shakespeare. Furthermore, they form the immediate prelude to his major pronouncement about the poet, which was to be, with the exception of the preface to *Zaïre* (1736) the last of this particular period of his life. The *Philosophical Letters*, or *Letters concerning the English Nation*, as their English title has it, constitute, in a sense, his farewell to objectivity about Shakespeare. After all, introducing his translation of "to be or not to be" he can still say "pardon the copy in favour of the original", and "when you see a translation, you are seeing only a feeble engraving of a beautiful picture". These precepts he was to forget later, as also his remarks about literal translation: "Do not think that I have rendered the English word for word; bad cess to the literal translators, who, in translating every word, weaken the sense! It is precisely in this that one can say that the letter kills, where the spirit vivifies."

However, let us consider, in this dying light of his appreciation of the bard, the translation that he now offers of "to be or not to be". His remark about literal translation is, in the immediate event, a *post factum* justification for turning the speech into alexandrines. We have seen his opinions about the necessity of rhyme. We have seen him regretting, in the case of French verse, the absence of tonic accent as opposed to measure. In the case of the French alexandrines there is also the compelling force of the twelve syllables, with their two hemistichs, which, combining with rhyme, seem to demand a close, antithetical form of thinking into which Voltaire's own prejudices and preconceptions flow, as into a ready-made mould. These facts become clearer with a juxtaposition of the two texts:

```
To be, or not to be; that is the question:              1
Whether 'tis nobler in the mind to suffer
The slings and arrows of outrageous fortune,
Or to take arms against a sea of troubles,
And by opposing end them? To die: to sleep;             5
No more; and, by a sleep to say we end
The heartache and the thousand natural shocks
That flesh is heir to, 'tis a consummation
Devoutly to be wished. To die, to sleep;
To sleep; perchance to dream: ay, there's the rub;      10
For in that sleep of death what dreams may come
When we have shuffled off this mortal coil,
Must give us pause. There's the respect
That makes calamity of so long a life;
For who would bear the whips and scorns of time,        15
The oppressor's wrong, the proud man's contumely,
The pangs of dispriz'd love, the law's delay,
The insolence of office, and the spurns
That patient merit of the unworthy takes,
```

When he himself might his quietus make   20
With a bare bodkin? who would fardels bear,
To grunt and sweat under a weary life,
But that the dread of something after death,
The undiscovered country from whose bourn
No traveller returns, puzzles the will,   25
And makes us rather bear those ills we have
Than fly to others that we know not of?
Thus conscience does make cowards of us all;
And thus the native hue of resolution
Is sicklied o'er with the pale cast of thought,   30
And enterprises of great pith and moment
With this regard their currents turn awry,
And lose the name of action. Soft you now!
The fair Ophelia! Nymph, in thy orisons
Be all my sins remember'd.   35

Voltaire

Demeure; il faut choisir, et passer à l'instant   1
De la vie à la mort, ou de l'être au néant.
Dieux cruels! s'il en est, éclairez mon courage.
Faut-il vieillir courbé sous la main qui m'outrage,
Supporter ou finir mon malheur et mon sort?   5
Qui suis-je? qui m'arrête? et qu'est-ce que la mort?
C'est la fin de nos maux, c'est mon unique asile;
Après de longs transports, c'est un sommeil tranquille;
On s'endort, et tout meurt. Mais un affreux réveil
Doit succéder peut-être aux douceurs du sommeil.   10
On nous menace, on dit que cette courte vie
De tourments éternels est aussitôt suivie.
O mort! Moment fatal! affreuse éternité!
Tout cœur à ton seul nom se glace, épouvanté.
Eh! qui pourrait, sans toi, supporter cette vie,   15
De nos prêtres menteurs bénir l'hypocrisie,
D'une indigne maîtresse encenser les erreurs,
Ramper sous un ministre, adorer ses hauteurs,
Et montrer les langueurs de son âme abattue
A des amis ingrats qui détournent la vue?   20
La mort serait trop douce en ces extrémités;
Mais le scrupule parle, et nous crie: "Arrêtez."
Il défend à nos mains cet heureux homicide,
Et d'un héros guerrier fait un chrétien timide, etc.[13]

Voltaire, we recollect, has already said that the Frenchman is frequently obliged to use four lines to express a thought for which the Englishman will use one. We next observe that he has translated the first twenty-
eight lines of Hamlet's soliloquy into twenty-four alexandrines. The
remainder (up to "Nymph in thy orisons/Be all my sins remember'd")
he chooses to ignore, dismissing it with an "etc." Why does he elect to
stop just here? A clue is perhaps to be found in lines 3 and 16 of the
translation. Why does Voltaire invoke the "dieux cruels" where Hamlet
does nothing of the sort? That such an invocation is normal and proper in
French tragedy when the protagonist reaches a height of suffering is a
possible answer, but a more plausible one is surely that the phrase permits

the following one, the anti-religious dig of "s'il en est". Line 16 of the
Voltaire version lends substance to such a view: Hamlet's inventory of the
disadvantages of this vale of tears is pretty exhaustive; but it leaves out
fawning upon the hypocrisy of lying priests, a defect remedied by the
translator again for his own purposes. This in its turn suggests that the anti-
clerical thread running through Voltaire's version can be brought to a
climax on his final couplet:

> Il défend à nos mains cet heureux homicide,
> Et d'un héros guerrier fait un chrétien timide.

Thus does the writer confer retrospectively upon the entire monologue an
undue preoccupation with religion, and import into it the attitudes of
eighteenth-century free-thinking. The would-be suicide, for Voltaire and
Voltaire's purposes, is an "heureux homicide" and an "héros guerrier".
It is not here that the Almighty has fixed his canon 'gainst self-slaughter in
the mind of the Prince of Denmark: indeed, Johnson, Dowden and others
seem to suggest that he is not meditating suicide at all.[14]

The pagan "Dieux cruels" of the beginning are in sharp contrast with
the "chrétien timide" of the end, and the reason again has little to do with
representing Shakespeare to the French people: the plural is a Voltairian
cover, and had to be used.

Thus, the adaptation is to some extent exploited for the purposes of
religious scepticism.

Line 1 of the English is rendered in the first two lines of the French.
The simple antithesis "to be or not to be" is prepared in the first line, "à
l'instant" being the merest padding to permit "néant" in line 2. Hamlet
could not be less concerned with acting on the instant: the word falsifies
his purpose, or lack of it. The couplet has an unmistakable ring of Corneille,
as has been noticed recently by Pons[15]: Lines 2, 3, 4, and 5 of the English
(with the exception of "to die, to sleep"), are represented by lines 3 to 5
in the French. The problem of the slings and arrows, and, in particular,
the taking of arms against the sea of troubles, are thrown aside: the
concrete, mediating imagery is removed and the whole expressed as a
positive, and above all, rational choice. Death, sleep and dreams are
inextricably interwoven at this stage in the reverie of Hamlet. They are
"unscrambled" as it were by the lucid Voltaire. Nevertheless, the shock of
"perchance to dream" after the repeated "to sleep" is not badly con-
strued in line 9 of the French: the combination of a regular (mid-line)
strong caesura, with the masculine rhyme "réveil/sommeil" giving
maximum prominence to réveil does not entirely betray this climax of the
soliloquy, but the translation of dream by "réveil" is amusing: to the
logical French philosopher either there is an after-life or there is not. If
there is, then death is not a dream but an awakening after the moment of
death. Lines 10, 11, 12, 13, and 14 of the French are equally amusing,
corresponding roughly as they do to Shakespeare's passage from line 10
("Ay, there's the rub") to line 14 inclusive, for in the English version

Hamlet is reflecting entirely on his own account, while, with Voltaire, it is others who inform us authoritatively (and they are, by implication, the priests) not that we may dream after death, but that we are in for eternal torments. Once more, were it not for the wicked bogey-priests (*"on* nous menace, *on* nous dit . . .") we could cheerfully make away with ourselves and sleep happily ever after.

"There's the respect that makes calamity of so long a life" is not attempted, being replaced by a direct invocation in lines 13 and 14 which does however lead Voltaire naturally into his translation of "who would bear the whips . . .". The strange thing about his inventory of the woes of this world, as opposed to Shakespeare's, is that this time it is Voltaire's which is expressed in the more concrete terms. The "prêtres menteurs" are a very concrete intrusion, "dispriz'd love" turns into "une indigne maîtresse",[16] "the insolence of office" appears as "Ramper sous un ministre, adorer ses hauteurs", and a troop of ungrateful friends have squeezed out the law's delay and the spurns that patient merit of the unworthy takes. It is a momentary and fascinating reversal of the habits of the two languages, for immediately afterwards, with Shakespeare, we are back among the bare bodkin and the fardels, the grunting and the sweating, and over all these unstage-like monstrosities Voltaire draws the veil of propriety by the single line "La mort serait trop douce en ces extrémités". He was not in the habit of tilting at windmills, or abstractions, and his own index of social evils to be fought on any occasion is simply transferred in great part to the mouth of the prince. The transference over, he returns to translating.

He has here added a note of militancy which increases the effect of energetic rationalizing emanating from the alexandrines. Shakespeare is betrayed by Voltaire the propagandist, and by the structure of the French verse. Hamlet's anguished reverie simply does not pierce through, and this is piquant in a translator who has readily granted that English poetry is more energetic than French. His original purpose is in any case high-lighted by his extraordinary substitution, in a later reprint of this rendering, of "Dieux cruels" by "Dieux justes". The change has nothing to do with Shakespeare, and a great deal to do with the brilliantly tactical Voltaire who, in ideological statements, had to avoid the gravamen of direct anti-clericalism. In the first version, the essential antecedent of "s'il en est" must be *dieux* and not *cruels*: it is excessive to suppose that Voltaire prefers to doubt the existence of cruelty in "Gods" rather than to doubt the existence of the "Gods" themselves. As between 1734 and 1761, however, it is not unreasonable to suppose that his own position had strengthened considerably, and at this time, he could venture "Dieux justes, s'il en est . . .", which has the paradoxical advantage of casting at one and the same time doubt upon the existence of God and upon the existence of His justice.

Be this as it may, we have here a Hamlet who, compared with the one that we know, and in spite of his Cornelian and rational weighing of the *pour* and the *contre*, seems vastly inclined to get on with the job; the English reader feels that he will be nicely finished within the twenty-four hours. This Hamlet is one whom time gallops withal. His whole tone is more oratorical, and he is a louder prince than ours. Thus couplets do make braggarts of us all.

In March 1761, Voltaire published his *Appel à toutes les Nations de l'Europe*, in which is to be found, added to his adaptation into verse of the soliloquy (containing the modification considered above), a prose version. He calls it a "traduction littérale", but adds afterwards that although it is scrupulous, it is not word for word.[17]

Voltaire's "literal" version

Etre ou n'être pas, c'est là la question,
S'il est plus noble dans l'esprit de souffrir
Les piqûres et les flèches de l'affreuse fortune,
Ou de prendre les armes contre une mer de trouble,
Et en s'opposant à eux, les finir? Mourir, dormir,   5
Rien de plus; et par ce sommeil, dire: Nous terminons
Les peines du cœur, et dix milles chocs naturels
Dont la chair est heritière; c'est une consommation
Ardemment désirable. Mourir, dormir:
Dormir! Peut-être rêver! Ah! voilà le mal.   10
Car, dans ce sommeil de la mort, quels rêves aura-t-on
Quand on a dépouillé cette enveloppe mortelle?
C'est là ce qui fait penser: c'est là la raison
Qui donne à la calamité une vie si longue.
Car qui voudrait supporter les coups, et les injures du temps,   15
Les torts de l'oppresseur, les dédains de l'orgueilleux,
Les angoisses d'un amour méprisé, les délais de la justice,
L'insolence des grandes places, et les rebuts
Que le mérite patient essuie de l'homme indigne?
Quand il peut faire son *quietus*[1]   20
Avec une simple aiguille à tête! Qui voudrait porter ces fardeaux,
Sangloter, suer sous une fatigante vie?
Mais cette crainte de quelque chose après la mort,
Ce pays ignoré, des bornes duquel
Nul voyageur revient, embarrasse la volonté,   25
Et nous fait supporter les maux que nous avons
Plutôt que de courir vers d'autres que nous ne connaissons pas:
Ainsi la conscience fait des poltrons de nous tous;
Ainsi la couleur naturelle de la résolution
Est ternie par les pâles teintes de la pensée;   30
Et les entreprises les plus importantes,
Par ce respect, tournent leur courant de travers,
Et perdent leur nom d'action ...

[1] Ce mot latin, qui signifie *tranquille*, est dans l'original.
(Note by Voltaire.)

Several comments of detail impose themselves. In line 3 he presumably confuses *slings* with *stings* since he translates *piqûres*. He can no doubt be excused for not having hit upon *field-gun* or *culverin*, both of which are given in Dover Wilson's glossary, for *slings*. Nor is *affreuse* particularly felicitous for *outrageous*. The "sea of troubles" he leaves to its fate in a

word-for-word translation,[18] and in any case no future French translator
was to settle it satisfactorily, their efforts consisting largely of attempts
first to analyse and then to expand the metaphor while retaining a
semblance of poetry. Thus, Dumas (1847) has

> la résignation
> ou la force luttant sur la mer orageuse
> et demandant le calme aux tempêtes?

Guizot (1821), correcting and revising Le Tourneur's edition, the preface
to which enraged Voltaire, returns to an "océan de maux" against which
Hamlet arms himself and fights "en y mettant un terme". Schwob has
"prendre les armes contre un océan de peines". Gide, in 1946, gives,
weakly, "mettre frein à une marée de douleurs", Pagnol (1947) "prendre
les armes" against "un océan d'ennuis". The last in line, Yves Bonnefoy,
quaintly enough, returns to the literal translation of Voltaire, which at
least suggests that the brutally mixed metaphor is not totally impossible
to the French contemporary poetic vision, whatever the Sorbonne might
think.[19] In line 7 of Voltaire, the thousand natural shocks have their
voltage multiplied tenfold, and the colloquialism of "there's the rub" is
avoided in "voilà le mal" (line 10). Here again, Bonnefoy was to be more
literal with "voilà où le bât le blesse", while Gide has the more clerkly
"c'est là le *hic*" (i.e. *hic jacet lepus*). The mortal coil was naturally to be a
nuisance; its contamination of *bustle* and "coil of rope" defeat modern
English and French alike. The nearest shot, according to Pons, is the
"quand nous avons secoué cet enlacis mortel" of Morand and Schwob.
Gide says, typically, *liens charnels*, and Pagnol "la guenille qui nous
enserre".

One conceives here and there that Voltaire may be sticking a little
unfairly to the word for word approach: Gide's "L'insolence des gens
officiels" is as literal as Voltaire's less thoughtful "l'insolence des grandes
places", while the force of *quietus*, a contamination of contemporary
meaning (account settled) and the past participle of *quiesco*, is missed
entirely, Voltaire seeing only the Latin meaning although he, and for that
matter his successors, should have had the French *quitte* and "en être
quitte pour . . ." under their noses. Here again we are in the presence of
an excess of literalism, and we cannot tell whether it is his ignorance or a
touch of malice which is reflected in his footnote to *quietus*. Immediately
afterwards, the translator's sense of the *bienséances* takes over, and "to
grunt" becomes the more nicely tragic "sangloter", where even the
delicate Gide gives us *geindre*. On the other hand, there is little to be done
with the French *conscience* in "conscience does make cowards of us all": it
is for the English-speaker of all time to learn, if he can, when by *conscience*
the French mean consciousness, and when conscience.

Yet the final impression is of a fair attempt to convey the original ring
of words of a great poet, and is in particular clinched by a direct plagiarism
on the part of Gide (whose translation is known for its exactitude) at the

end: for "their currents turn awry" Gide borrows Voltaire's "tournent leurs courants de travers".

Voltaire, in his own time, had remarked that all Englishmen know this speech by heart. Nothing short of some linguistic pre-frontal lobotomy could excise from the mind of the English-speaking reader the direct resonances of the original which arise from Voltaire's translation and while one is all too ready, officially, to concede that they obfuscate the real enormities of the French as it stands, secretly, it is almost impossible not to accept this version as superior to the philosopher's alexandrines, sea of troubles or no.[20]

This was probably the last occasion on which Voltaire was to use the literal translation for purposes of serious literary investigation. Later, he was to employ it to thrust down the gullets of a European public the barbarities of the bard. The rest of the story has been most adequately told, and I at least have nothing to add to it: there is a silence of nearly a decade after the *Appel à toutes les Nations de l'Europe*, then the tangle with Walpole in 1768. The cult of Shakespeare in Europe had however been gaining slow ground during this time, from 1745 at least, with the first volume of La Place's *Théâtre Anglais*, through Ducis's malversation of *Hamlet* in 1769 (to be followed by others by the same hand) and so to the more serious attempt of Le Tourneur in 1776.[21] It is significant that it should be the more literal attempt of Le Tourneur which incensed Voltaire, and, in particular, the excessive praise bestowed upon Shakespeare in the preface. From then on, Voltaire abandoned any serious attempt at an appreciation as he went deliberately to war on behalf, as he claims, of his nation, against Shakespeare and the English. After all, a cult of Shakespeare was not at all what he, the successor of Racine, had intended when (the first in Europe, as he never tired of saying) he pointed out the diamonds in this dung-heap. He had heard that the youth of Paris were for Shakespeare: the English stage scaffolds and the English stage brothels were winning the day over the plays of Racine and the finest scenes of Corneille.[22] Just as the *Appel à toutes les Nations* had been a tongue-in-cheek appeal to some sort of final judgment of the nations as between Corneille, Racine, Shakespeare and by implication Voltaire, so the correspondence of 1776 moves naggingly towards a final crushing judgment, or so he hoped, from the highest literary court of appeal in the realm, the Académie Française, from whom he expressly expected some sort of verdict such as had been meted out to Corneille's *Le Cid*. To this end, as Lounsbury has said,[23] "he had carefully culled out from the mass of Shakespeare's writings everything he knew which would be offensive to his audience". When d'Alembert, the secretary of the Academy, pointed out that some of these were perhaps too shocking to be read in genteel company, Voltaire suggested the following gambit:

Serait-il mal de s'arrêter à ces petits défilés, de passer le mot en lisant, et de faire désirer au public qu'on le prononçât, afin de laisser voir le divin Skakespeare dans toute son horreur et dans son incroyable bassesse?[24]

No doubt, on that day of Saint Louis in 1776, Voltaire scored some sort of triumph when d'Alembert read his diatribe in an open session of the Academy. Yet the ultimate victory was with William Shakespeare. Voltaire acted out of complete sincerity in his attack: he had never intended to inform Europe that there were anything more than isolated beauties in the works, and the effect of Le Tourneur's introduction deifying Shakespeare evoked the panicky wrath of a sorcerer's apprentice. The inevitable result of Voltaire's final attack was to focus on the works that gaze of Europe which, in the surge of pre-romanticism, was already half turned in the right direction.

Yet this was not its most important effect. For half a century the greatest man of letters in Europe had intermittently called the attention of the continent to Shakespeare in the most combative manner. He had, and especially towards the end of his career, presented Shakespearian tragedy and French classical tragedy (including, we were to understand, his own) as alternatives, though in the earlier period he had regretted two things: that some of the energy and virility of English blank verse could not be infused into French tragedy, and that Shakespeare had not been born in the age of Addison. His own translations, for whatever purpose he translated, tend to support him in the former view, and he often intended that they should support the latter. Basically, he could not translate Shakespeare because he could not transform Voltaire, and the thought never occurred to him.

In short, and with the exception of the more extreme expressions of the Romantic movement, Voltaire exhausted the aesthetic necessity of a choice between Shakespearian and Racinian tragedy, although such attitudes continued for long enough, and indeed intensified during the Revolution and Empire, for chauvinistic reasons. In this historical function he performed an unintentional but signal service to European literature. Stendhal's *Racine et Shakespeare*, similar works, and similar romantic attitudes such as the war-cry "Shakespeare est un dieu et Racine un polisson" drain away in their turn the possibility of a choice opposite to that of Voltaire, and thus is the way opened for a more balanced view of the bard. The spate of translations and productions in the nineteenth and twentieth centuries is sufficient proof of this, and the movement has been on the whole towards the more literal rendering.[25]

All this, from Voltaire's own point of view, adds up no doubt to a defeat, though a minor one: he was ultimately defeated in so little else. He saw the rising vogue of Shakespeare as an unhappy epilogue to his days: "Je vais mourir en laissant la France barbare. . . ."[26] It may be said that he was hardly defeated by the Shakespearian cult in his own day, whatever he may have thought at the last. His major excuse for Shakespeare was that the poet was a prisoner of the barbarous Elizabethan age, and the excuse of imprisonment in an age must be his own too: the vast majority of Europe agreed with Voltaire while he was alive. Shakespeare has been justified, for the French people, by history, though not perhaps by the history of the French language: the seeds from which the phenomenolo-gical, introspective world-view has sprung were planted in the French Romantic movement, and have flowered sensationally in the work of Sartre and Camus. In an age when Sartre echoes in his title *L'Etre et le Néant*, the phrase that Voltaire chooses for Hamlet, in an age when Camus, in *Le mythe de Sisyphe*, can posit the very problem of life as the problem of suicide, we can see why Frenchmen want to take another look at "to be or not to be".

There is, in the Court Room of the University of Aberdeen, a picture by Sir Joshua Reynolds, in which we may see the modest and kindly Aberdeen philosopher, Dr. James Beattie, jerked into prominence by the recent President of the Royal Academy, clutching a copy of his *Essay on Truth*, the while an Angel of Truth holds down the head of Voltaire, who is accompanied by other assorted sceptics. Had Reynolds substituted Shakespeare for Beattie, his canvas would have stated a near-truth instead of a hilarious absurdity.

NOTES

1. Although as regards measure, the French alexandrine is considerably more elastic than is always apparent to the English scholar.
2. A. Lacroix, *L'influence de Shakespeare sur le théâtre français jusqu'à nos jours* (Brussels, 1856). Jean-Jules Jusserand, *Shakespeare en France sous l'ancien régime* (Paris, 1898). Thomas R. Lounsbury, *Shakespeare and Voltaire* (London, 1902). F. Baldensperger, *Etudes d'histoire littéraire, 2e série* (Paris, 1910). See also Mary-Margaret H. Barr, *A Bibliography of Writings on Voltaire, 1825-1925* (New York, 1929), pp. 48-50, F. C. Green, *Minuet* (London, 1935), and G. Bonno, *La culture et la civilisation britanniques devant l'opinion française de la paix d'Utrecht aux L ttres philosophiques* (Philadelphia, 1948).
3. Shakespeare is mentioned earlier than this by Voltaire in his *Essai sur la poésie épique* of 1728 (French version) and in his preface to his tragedy of *Oedipe* in 1730. Many of the references to Shakespeare in the works of Voltaire were listed for me by Dr. John Carr of the University of Glasgow, in 1957, and I am happy to express my debt to him. I would also like to thank Messrs. Brumfitt and Taylor of the University of St. Andrews for many helpful suggestions.
4. Jean-Jules Jusserand, *Shakespeare en France sous l'Ancien Régime* (Paris, 1898). Generally speaking, it is in vain that one follows the French tourist of the time to Britain in the hope of some notice of Shakespeare. The birds that some of them see are indeed curious, though there is no swan of Avon. One of the travellers, Father Huc in 1654, penetrated as far north as Buchan (Buquhan) where, he informs us, ". . . no rats are propagated . . . and if you bring one in from elsewhere, it cannot live . . . you also find there birds called *clayks*, whose birth is amazing in that they are the produce of trees, occurring on the sea-shore, and, like fruits, falling into the sea when they are ripe; so much so that one can find branches laden with these unfinished products, some of which have as

yet only their beaks and heads formed, others have half their bodies finished, and others still, ready to fly or swim, hold on to the tree only by a tiny thread, the which being broken, these aquatic birds fly and swim like ducks." (I am indebted to Professor V. C. Wynne-Edwards for the information that this is one of the variants of the barnacle goose myth, and it is interesting to note that the legend is propagated in north Scotland, though in a rather different version, essentially by Hector Boece, first principal of Aberdeen University.) Cf. Edward Heron-Allen, F.R.S., *Barnacles in Nature and Myth* (London, 1928). (Ref. also supplied by Professor Wynne-Edwards.)

5. Jusserand, *op. cit.* pp. 130-49.

6. *Op. cit.* pp. 46-47.

7. There is a recent, level-headed summary of the process in F. A. Taylor's edition of the *Lettres Philosophiques* (Basil Blackwell, Oxford, 1961), n. 3 to letter XVIII. He follows the line taken by Baldensperger, *op. cit.* p. 170; it is not a *volte-face* on Voltaire's part but a change of "weighting" as between the concepts *barbare* and *génie*.

8. Cf. F. A. Taylor, *op. cit.*, introduction, pp. xi and xii.

9. Vol. 2, p. 312 of the collected works as published (after Beuchot's text) in the collection *Grands Ecrivains de la France* (1877). All references are to this edition unless otherwise stated.

10. Quoted by H. H. Furness Jr. in *A New Variorum Edition of Shakespeare*, Vol. XVII (Philadelphia, 1913).

11. He had not yet, of course, in his library, J. and P. Knapton's eight-volume edition of the works, which was to appear in 1747, so had not the advantage of Pope's and Warburton's comments. But he probably had already volume 6 of Tonson's edition of 1714. (Items 3161 and 3160 respectively of *Biblioteka Voltera: Katalog Knig*, Moscow-Leningrad, 1961.)

12. *Cato* had been translated into French, and was much admired for its "regularity". In his witch hunt for the improper image in English poetry, it is then not too surprising that from amongst Addison's deal of exceptionally blank verse, Voltaire should fail to single out for adverse comment one of the more interesting figures in the play: ". . . the corpse of half her Senate / Manure the fields of Thessaly . . ."

13. A brief comparison of these two versions is to be found in a short article by C. Serrurier, in *Neophilologus* (1920), pp. 205 ff.; the author appears to be unaware of Lounsbury's volume, as does Baldensperger, writing eight years after its publication.

14. Cf. Dover Wilson's edition of the play, n. 56 to Act III, scene i.

15. Christian Pons, "Les traductions de Hamlet", in *Shakespeare en France* (*Etudes Anglaises*, XIIIe année, No. 2, Avril-Juin, 1960). M. Pons's article is the latest study of this topic and the entire volume is of the greatest interest. It should be added that under the heading "Art dramatique" in his *Dictionnaire philosophique* Voltaire rewrites the couplet, and in this revision the development is prepared of the choice "to suffer . . . to end": "Demeure, il faut choisir de l'être ou du néant. / Ou souffrir ou périr c'est là ce qui m'attend."

16. Serrurier's suspicion (*op. cit.* p. 208) that the "indigne maîtresse" is in fact the Church seems exaggerated.

17. ". . . qui ne peut rendre le mot propre anglais par le mot propre français . . . ."

18. Though it does not leave *him*: the French *trouble* was not in 1761 the English *troubles*, and is not now.

19. All the above translations are quoted from Christian Pons (*op. cit.*), who himself suggests "Ou s'il n'est pas préférable de prendre les armes

et de partir en guerre contre la tempête, contre l'ouragan, et contre l'océan, pour ainsi dire, contre l'infini de nos petits malheurs". Bonnefoy, on the other hand, rejoices aggressively in his retention of the mixed metaphor: "Il est beau d'oser écrire *et de prendre les armes contre une mer de troubles*." (Cited by Pons, *op. cit.* p. 128.)

20. We have seen that Bonnefoy rejoices in the word-for-word version of that metaphor, in 1957. In 1960 Pons cannot agree: "La langue française ne permet pas de prendre les armes contre une mer, encore moins contre une mer de troubles; et le mot anglais *trouble* ne veut pas dire trouble. Je regrette que Bonnefoy ait cru devoir conserver cette fausse audace dans sa propre traduction." *Op. cit. loc. cit.*

21. In the fifteenth edition of the *Encyclopédie*, in 1765, under the article Stratford-on-Avon, the chevalier de Jaucourt, in the course of a five-columned article, can write "génie sublime, le plus grand qu'on connaisse dans la poésie dramatique".

22. Vol. 50, p. 64, Letter to M. le comte d'Argental, 30 July 1776. *Echafauds* I take to be a reference to executions on the stage, in contradistinction to Lounsbury, who interprets the words "échafauds anglais" as "the English boards".

23. *Op. cit.* p. 372.

24. Vol. 50, p. 68, Letter to d'Alembert.

25. It has been noted that two contemporary Frenchmen differ diametrically as to whether "prendre les armes contre une mer de trouble" will, or will not (or should, or should not), get past a French audience. The English spectator of Shakespeare-in-French certainly cannot prevent the French from becoming a mere mnemonic for the English text, and the more literal the French text the more will this happen. I found it to be particularly the case with Gide's translation of *Hamlet*, produced by Jean-Louis Barrault at the Marigny on 17 October 1946. Nor was my reaction significantly different eleven years later with Maurice Jacquemont's production, in the translation of Suzanne Bing and Jacques Copeau at the theatre festival of Sarlat in 1957.

In the number of *Etudes Anglaises* already referred to, there are eleven articles dealing more or less directly with modern French productions of Shakespeare. The reader may also consult the catalogue of the exhibition *Mises en scène de Shakespeare et des élisabéthains en France, d'Antoine à nos jours*, organized by Jean Jacquot at the Institut Pédagogique National, 29, rue d'Ulm, Paris 5e, 1960.

26. Vol. 50, p. 64. Letter to d'Argental, 30 July 1776.

William Witte

DEUS ABSCONDITUS

Shakespeare in Eighteenth-Century Germany

The impact of Shakespeare on German writers in the last decades of the eighteenth century came with the force of a quasi-divine revelation. In their references to Shakespeare, German authors and critics of that period again and again fall back upon the language of religious experience, as if that were the only appropriate form of expression.[1] One salient feature which the revelation of Shakespeare's genius has in common with scriptural revelation is its paradoxical character: what it reveals, as an object of faith and adoration, is a mystery; the core of what it proclaims remains hidden, ineffable, incommensurable.

The first preacher of the new gospel was Herder. Before him, Shakespeare had been rejected by Gottsched, translated (after a fashion) by Wieland, defended against ill-informed criticism by Gerstenberg, vindicated by Lessing. Herder's essay on Shakespeare [2] strikes an entirely new note; he speaks not as a judge but as a prophet, testifying to the faith that is in him. His style is rhapsodical; his essay is a panegyric—a panegyric, however, which is full of acute critical insight. He sees Shakespeare as the creator of a complete and self-sufficient world of his own: "God of drama, for whom no clock strikes on steeple or temple, but who has to create space and the measure of time". . . . "The whole world is merely a body for this great spirit: all scenes of nature are limbs of this body, just as all characters and modes of thought are features of this spirit—and the whole may be called that giant God of Spinoza: Pan, the Universe!" The concluding sentences of the essay are addressed to Goethe; Herder speaks of him (without explicitly mentioning his name) as the friend whom he "had more than once embraced before the sacred image" of Shakespeare, and acclaims Goethe's project of rearing a monument to Shakespeare in the shape of a play on a theme from Germany's era of chivalry.

That Herder's mantle as the prophet of the dramatic messiah had fallen on Goethe is evident, both in the play to which Herder refers—*Götz von Berlichingen*—and in his speech *Zum Shakespeares-Tag*, which formed part of the "liturgy" (the word is Goethe's own [3]) used by a gathering of devotees who had assembled at Goethe's home to do homage to Shakespeare. Goethe's brief encomium is much slighter than Herder's essay;

nevertheless it is a moving profession of faith, faith in a being of godlike power, a thaumaturge: "The first page of Shakespeare that I read made me his for life; and when I had finished reading the first of his plays, I stood like a man born blind to whom a miracle-working hand suddenly gives his sight. I realized, I felt most vividly that my existence was infinitely enlarged, all was new to me, unknown, and the unfamiliar light hurt my eyes." Perhaps the convert was protesting too much at that stage, as converts are apt to do; but if in later life he no longer felt capable of such complete self-surrender, at any rate he was never ashamed to own his Shakespearian allegiance. In a short poem (published in 1820), in which he harks back to the years before his visit to Italy, his worship of Shakespeare—"William! star of loveliest height!"—is linked with his love for Charlotte von Stein: these two forces, he claims, have made him what he is.

> Einer Einzigen angehören,
> Einen Einzigen verehren,
> Wie vereint es Herz und Sinn!
> Lida! Glück der nächsten Nähe,
> William! Stern der schönsten Höhe,
> Euch verdank' ich, was ich bin.

In his essay *Shakespeare und kein Ende!* (1813), Shakespeare appears as the spirit of the universe, the World Soul grown articulate and revealing secrets which normally remain impenetrable: "the secret must come out, supposing the stones should have to reveal it. Even inanimate nature crowds in, all subordinate things join in the dialogue, the elements, phenomena of sky, earth and sea, thunder and lightning, wild animals raise their voices." And in his middle seventies he speaks of Shakespeare, in one of his conversations with Eckermann (30th March 1824), as "a being of a higher order, to whom I look up and whom I have to revere".

Schiller, ten years younger than Goethe, fifteen years younger than Herder, grew up in a literary environment which had largely accepted the new gospel. He became familiar with a number of Shakespeare's plays at an early stage in his education; but the more eagerly he studied them, the more mysterious and inaccessible their creator appeared to him. Many years later he recorded his early reaction in the essay *On Naive and Reflective Poetry* (1795), in which Shakespeare figures as the modern archetype of the Naive—genius at one with nature. "Like the Deity behind the structure of the universe, so he stands behind his works; he is his works, and his works are himself." The god of drama whom Herder had invoked, the creator of his own world, is felt to be an immanent deity, elusive and inscrutable. Schiller might have made his point in the words of Isaiah (xlv. 15): "Verily thou art a God that hidest thyself."

The wise old hero of Lessing's *Nathan* holds [4] that a man's devotion, his acceptance of the will of God, does not depend upon his theories about the nature of God; the operation of grace is not conditional upon theological opinion. The same applies, *mutatis mutandis*, in the sphere of literature. The influence of a great writer does not depend on fullness of understanding, depth of insight, or correctness of appreciation. While trying to follow in his footsteps, those who come after him may be taking an entirely different route: but his influence may remain potent just the same. An author, like anybody else, can only become what he has it in him to be; he will be receptive to certain stimuli, impervious to others. He can be affected by what he finds in another man's work only in so far as something in his own nature responds to it; in absorbing an influence from outside, he will adapt it to his own potentialities, thus transforming what he receives. The more creative and original the recipient, the more thoroughgoing this process of transformation is likely to be. Goethe put the point memorably in the first of his *Epistles*. Every reader, he says, finds his own self in what he is reading, and if he is a powerful spirit, he will project himself into the book, amalgamating the alien elements with his own being:

> Liest doch nur jeder
> Aus dem Buch sich heraus, und ist er gewaltig, so liest er
> In das Buch sich hinein, amalgamiert sich das Fremde.

It is a matter of common consent that among the leaders of the literary revival in eighteenth-century Germany, Goethe and Schiller felt the influence of Shakespeare most and that they show it most clearly in their own works. How, then, did it operate? What is the nature of their discipleship, and what conception of the Master do their writings reveal?

As one would expect, there is little direct borrowing. Neither Goethe nor Schiller was interested in plagiarizing; both, no doubt, had pondered Lessing's trenchant remarks about Shakespeare's immunity against plagiarism: "It has been said that it would be easier to wrest his club from Hercules than to filch a line from Homer, and this applies in the fullest sense to Shakespeare too. The least of his beauties bears an imprint which at once proclaims to the whole world: 'I am Shakespeare's!' ... Shakespeare requires to be studied, not plundered." [5] It is true that in one of his conversations with Eckermann (18th January 1825), Goethe pleaded guilty to having appropriated a song of Shakespeare's and put it in the mouth of Mephistopheles in *Faust I* (lines 3682 ff.), the song in question being Ophelia's "Tomorrow is Saint Valentine's day". "And why not?", Goethe added, in a spirit of banter and bravado; "why should I bother to invent one of my own, if Shakespeare's was just right and said precisely what was required?" A poet of Goethe's originality can afford to take such a cavalier view of literary property, once in a while. In any case, the "plagiarism" is slight; Goethe's version of the song pictures the same general situation, but only two or three lines distinctly echo Shakespeare's.

Imitation of Shakespeare's manner, on the other hand, as distinct from specific borrowings, is a marked feature both of Goethe's and of Schiller's early plays; what Herder had said about *Götz von Berlichingen*— that it was to be a monument to Shakespeare —applies with equal force to Schiller's *Räuber*. In his *Götz*, Goethe frankly adopts what he conceives to be the Shakespearian technique: short scenes, full of action and movement; frequent changes of scene, giving a restless, kaleidoscopic effect; a wealth of episodes; mingling of humour and tragedy; liberal use of crowd and battle scenes; drastic realism in the delineation of character, and a vigorous, racy turn of phrase which does not shrink from occasional coarseness (as witness the hero's famous but unprintable exclamation in Act III). It is true that he adapts this technique to his own characteristically autobiographical mode of writing; in depicting the miserable fate of Weislingen, the faithless lover, he was, on his own admission,[6] castigating himself, and in that sense *Götz*, too, forms (to use his own celebrated phrase) a fragment of that great confession which makes up the sum-total of his works.[7] Even so, his friend and mentor Herder felt that the young poet had come to grief by trying to out-Shakespeare Shakespeare; he dismissed the first (1771) version of the play with the cutting remark: "Shakespeare has completely spoilt you."

As for Schiller's *Räuber*, the author himself points out, in his own analysis of the play, that the dominant traits in the hero's character had been amalgamated in his imagination "after the manner of Shakespeare", and he adds: "If the beauties of his play do not show that the author is infatuated with Shakespeare, his extravagances betray it all the more clearly." The beginnings of this infatuation can be traced back as far as 1776, when J. F. Abel, one of Schiller's favourite teachers at the Stuttgart Military Academy, used quotations from *Othello* to illustrate some points in a lecture on psychology. As soon as the class was over, young Schiller asked to be allowed to borrow the book; and the frequent references to Shakespeare in his early writings show how eagerly he had studied Shakespeare's works. Among those early writings is his medico-philosophical dissertation on the mind-body problem (*On the connection between the physical and the spiritual in man's nature*; 1780), in which he takes his case histories from *Julius Caesar*, *Macbeth*, and *Richard III* and in which he affectionately refers to their author as "our Shakespeare": the god of drama whom Herder had invoked transcends national frontiers, being acknowledged and claimed as their own by worshippers everywhere.

If Schiller admits having taken a leaf out of Shakespeare's book in his portrayal of Karl Moor, the sublime criminal, the pedigree of the villain of the piece is even more patently Shakespearian. Franz Moor's kinship with Iago and Richard III would be sufficiently obvious, even if Schiller had not made a point of calling attention to it. But would Iago and Richard acknowledge this German cousin? A certain general family resemblance is evident. Like Iago, Franz takes a cynical pleasure in seeing wickedness triumphant. "Who will now come and dare call me to account? or tell me to my face: you are a villain?" he asks, (II. 2), echoing Iago's soliloquy (II. 3) "And what's he then that says I play the villain?" But the similarity does not go very far, or very deep. Franz lacks Iago's animal spirits, his vitality, his soldierly robustness; time always seems to hang heavy on his hands; one cannot imagine him saying, as Iago does,

"Pleasure and action make the hours seem short". Both men are quick-witted, but Iago's mind is essentially practical; he reacts promptly to circumstances as they arise, improvising his intrigue as he goes along:

'Tis here, but yet confus'd:
Knavery's plain face is never seen till us'd.

He has little time for introspection and self-analysis; his thinking is geared to action. Not so Franz Moor, whom his creator describes as an intellectual, philosophizing villain. In several lengthy monologues he develops, not only (like Iago) his plan of action but his philosophy of life and conduct.[8] Iago is a serpent that stings because it is in its nature to sting. Franz cannot act without rationalizing his action. He needs a creed, however perverse, to guide him, and when in the end his philosophy of moral nihilism fails him, he collapses. This brooding self-consciousness in the pursuit of evil distinguishes him from Richard III, as it does from Iago. In both cases, outward similarities mask a fundamental difference. Like Richard, Franz Moor is physically ugly; both men bear nature a grudge, and resolve to assert themselves against a world which prizes beauty and recoils from ugliness. Where they cannot hope to win affection, they are determined to attain power, whatever the cost. Queen Margaret's description of Richard—"the slave of nature and the son of hell"—fits Franz equally well. And yet the expository monologues in which the two characters speak of their ill-favoured appearance reveal very different attitudes. Richard states the fact that he has been "cheated of feature by dissembling nature" as a simple fact, to be accepted, not indeed without bitterness, but without argument, and he goes on to say how he proposes to deal with the situation:

And therefore, since I cannot prove a lover,
To entertain these fair well-spoken days,
I am determined to prove a villain . . .

In a parallel context, Franz Moor does not content himself with a statement of fact; he insists on asking why nature should have put him at such an unfair disadvantage—a question which concerns the moral structure of the world[9]: "Why did nature have to saddle me with this burden of ugliness? Why me, of all people? . . . Who has authorized her to deny me what she bestowed on him? Why did she go to work with such partiality?"

This shift of emphasis from what is to what ought to be shows the disciple of Shakespeare remaking the object of his cult in his own image, the "naive" being transformed into the "reflective," to use the terminology of Schiller's essay. It has been suggested that the causes of this transformation lay in the social and political conditions of eighteenth-century Germany—in the arid political life of the German duodecimo states, so cramped and stunted in comparison with the buccaneering vigour of Elizabethan England; in a petty tyranny and a restrictive social system under which writers, driven in upon themselves, rebelled in imagination against the oppressive reality of their existence.[10] Such connections between the literary life of a period and its social and political background are hard to establish with any final certainty.[11] But whatever the explanation—sociological or purely personal, or both—it is clear that in the very act of doing homage to Shakespeare, both Goethe and Schiller were beginning to work out their literary salvation in their own way. A contemporary reviewer, one C. F. Timme, hailed the author of *Die Räuber* as a German reincarnation of Shakespeare: "If ever we may look for a German Shakespeare, here he is." It is easy to point out, with the wisdom of hindsight, that this prophecy did not come true, and that it would not have come true even if Schiller had gone on writing in his early vein. It is equally easy to dismiss Timme's enthusiasm with a sneer, as Coleridge dismissed a comparison between Milton and Klopstock, muttering to himself, when his German host told him "that Klopstock was the German Milton"—"a very *German* Milton indeed!!!"[12] Such mockery, however, would involve an *ignoratio elenchi*, seeking to prove what has never been denied; for Timme's phrase "a German Shakespeare"—a kind of oxymoron—does not ignore the difference between the two authors, but rather emphasizes it.

Recalling some of the companions of his youth in his autobiography, Goethe remarks: "We revered Shakespeare to the point of adoration."[13] "I joyfully confessed that something higher was hovering above me; this affected my friends, who all gave themselves up to this way of thinking."[14] If there is exaltation in such an encounter with a quasi-divine spirit, there is also apprehension: a fear akin to that which—as the history of religious experience shows—overcomes the believer in the divine presence, and makes him want to hide or run away. Again and again we see the elect of God shrinking from the demands which total commitment would lay upon them: Moses hiding his face at the sight of the burning bush and protesting, "Who am I, that I should go unto Pharaoh?"; Isaiah crying out, "Woe is me, for I am undone"; Jonah taking ship to Tarshish; the rich young man in the gospel story going away grieved. Commitment involves self-abnegation, surrender of the disciple's personality. The apostle who proudly claims "I laboured more abundantly than they all" immediately adds the all-important qualification: "yet not I, but the grace of God which was with me."[15]

However sincere Goethe's and Schiller's Shakespeare-worship, the sacrifice involved in this kind of self-surrender proved too great. All the world agrees (Goethe says in one of his Suleika poems) that any loss can be borne so long as we are allowed to remain ourselves:

> Jedes Leben sei zu führen,
> Wenn man sich nicht selbst vermisst;
> Alles könne man verlieren,
> Wenn man bliebe, was man ist.

Or, as Schiller puts it in his review of Bürger's poems: "All that the poet can give us is his individuality." His individuality, the source of his creative power, must be preserved—even at the price of apostasy. Goethe analyses this act of artistic self-preservation in one of his conversations with Eckermann (25th December 1825), and what he has to say on the subject might be summed up in Macbeth's words: "under him/My genius is rebuk'd": "Shakespeare is altogether too rich and powerful. Any creative artist must not read more than one of his plays every year if he does not want to be ruined by him. I did well to get rid of him by writing my *Götz* and *Egmont*. . . . Shakespeare gives us golden apples in silver vessels. By studying his works we do indeed obtain the silver bowl, but we have only got potatoes to put in it, that's the trouble!"

Bracketing *Götz* and *Egmont* in these reminiscent remarks, Goethe marks out two phases in his Shakespeare cult—discipleship and emancipation: the first flush of enthusiasm in *Götz* (1771-3), and a withdrawal from tutelage in *Egmont* (begun in 1775, completed in 1787). *Götz* exemplifies the imitation of Shakespearian technique [16]; the reference to *Egmont*, on the other hand, calls attention to the intensely Goethean theme of the play. Egmont resembles his creator in that his nature exhibits the working of a mysterious force which Goethe calls "daemonic"; Goethe's description of this strange phenomenon in his autobiography [17] clearly shows the play to be rooted in intimate personal experience. Characters like Egmont, driven by an irresistible inner compulsion, cannot accept guidance from others. The hero of the play cannot find it in his heart to take another man's advice at a critical moment; he has to follow his own bent, whatever the risk. It is in the context of his observations on the "daemonic" that Goethe quotes "that strange but tremendous saying: Nemo contra deum nisi deus ipse" which he chose as a motto for Part IV of his autobiography. Commenting on it in conversation with Riemer (3rd July 1810), he remarked: "God always encounters Himself. God in man meets Himself yet again in man; wherefore no one has cause to disparage himself, even compared with the greatest." Here is the key to the apparent paradox of Goethe's attitude to Shakespeare: involvement and withdrawal, self-surrender and self-assertion, the god without confronted by the *daimon* within—a striking example of that polarity which formed a fundamental pattern of Goethe's experience and of his thinking.

This polarity may also be discerned in Goethe's best-known contribution to Shakespeare studies, the analysis of *Hamlet* in his novel *Wilhelm Meister's Apprenticeship*. The hero of the novel, who has joined a company of players, is introduced to Shakespeare's drama by a man of taste and discernment, and falls completely under its spell. When, later on, a performance of *Hamlet* is decided upon, he is chosen to play the lead, and in the course of preparation and rehearsal he gives his fellow-actors a detailed interpretation of the play. According to his reading of it, the key to Hamlet's conduct lies in the words

> The time is out of joint; O cursed spite,
> That ever I was born to set it right!

"It is clear to me", he comments, "that what Shakespeare wanted to depict is this: a great deed laid upon a soul who is not equal to it. . . . Here an oak sapling is planted in a precious jar which should have been filled only with lovely flowers; the roots spread, the jar is shattered. A beautiful, pure, noble, and most moral being, lacking the strength of nerve that makes a hero, perishes under a burden which he can neither bear nor throw off." [18] Nowadays this conception of an unheroic, sentimental Hamlet is fairly generally discredited. A. C. Bradley rejects it; so does Dover Wilson; so does A. A. Jack; so does Allardyce Nicoll; so does T. S. Eliot[19]; and indeed it is difficult to square it with the text. How is it that Goethe so radically misread a work to the study of which he had given much time and thought? The answer would seem to be that the interpretation propounded in *Wilhelm Meister* suits—and fits—the character who propounds it. Goethe's Wilhelm, a likeable but somewhat indecisive sort of person, projects himself into the part he is about to act; "the same mind that was satisfied with the unsatisfactoriness, except as a personality, of his own hero might not unnaturally have read into Shakespeare's what he did".[20] The Prince whose character Wilhelm Meister expounds so eloquently is Goethe's Hamlet rather than Shakespeare's, and the relevant passages in the novel are, in Gundolf's words, "a monument to Shakespeare, as a God to whom Goethe had sacrificed, and at the same time a monument to his newly won freedom".[21]

In Schiller's case there is no such ambiguous oblation, commemorating both dedication and release. Schiller could not have claimed, as Goethe did, that in writing his early plays he had got Shakespeare out of his system. He remains spellbound, marvelling all the time at Shakespeare's superhuman stature: "Why do I feel so dizzy, even yet", he exclaims in a letter to his friend Huber (5th October 1785), "when I look up at the giant Shakespeare!" Various episodes in his earlier plays show that he continues to model himself on the Master. The hero's beast fable in *Fiesco* recalls Menenius Agrippa's "pretty tale" about the belly and the other organs of the body in *Coriolanus*, while the patter of the Moor reminds one of such characters as Launcelot Gobbo in *The Merchant of Venice* or Autolycus in *The Winter's Tale*. Ferdinand's *crime passionnel* in *Kabale und Liebe*, prompted by "a jealousy so strong/That judgment cannot cure", owes something to *Othello*. The heart of the infante in *Don Carlos* beats in tune with the author's own, but he has "the soul of Hamlet"[22]; he, too, seeks to hide a terrible secret from all those who would pluck out the heart of his mystery; like Hamlet, Schiller's young Prince, "the expectancy and rose of the fair state", grows melancholy and shows occasional traces of an antic disposition.

These Shakespearian parallels are plain. Others, however, are strangely elusive. There is, for instance, a group of scenes in *Don Carlos* which centres round King Philip (III. 1-4): having been led to suspect that his queen is deceiving him with Carlos, his son by his first marriage, to whom she had originally been betrothed, Philip is a prey to doubt and jealousy. The general pattern of these scenes—the intriguers working on their victim with vicious relish—suggests an analogy with *Othello*, III. 3, and so do some verbal echoes, such as Domingo's speech

> Guter Name
> Ist das kostbare, einzge Gut, um welches
> Die Königin mit einem Bürgerweibe
> Wetteifern muss—

which closely resembles Iago's

> Good name in man or woman, dear my lord,
> Is the immediate jewel of their souls:

or Alba's seeming reluctance to disclose to the King what even a slave may keep to himself, his secret thoughts, which is modelled on Iago's

> Good my lord, pardon me;
> Though I am bound to every act of duty,
> I am not bound to that all slaves are free to.
> Utter my thoughts?

At the same time, some of Schiller's lines bear a striking resemblance to corresponding passages in *The Winter's Tale*, I. 2. The King's angry resentment at the thought that his dishonour is (as he imagines) common knowledge, and that he is the last to find out:

> They're here with me already, whispering, rounding
> 'Sicilia is a so-forth.' 'Tis far gone,
> When I shall gust it last;

the reproaches which he levels at Camillo:

> or else thou must be counted
> A servant grafted in my serious trust,
> And therein negligent; or else a fool
> That seest a game play'd home, the rich stake drawn,
> And tak'st it all for jest;

Camillo's indignation when his master reveals the nature of his suspicion:

> I would not be a stander-by, to hear
> My sovereign mistress clouded so, without
> My present vengeance taken:

all these are parallelled in Schiller's play. Yet there is no corroborative evidence to show that Schiller knew *The Winter's Tale*, apart from a general resemblance between Autolycus and the Moor in *Fiesco*, which is too vague to be conclusive; there is no reference to the play either in Schiller's correspondence or in his critical writings.[23] The parallels, close though they are, might conceivably be fortuitous. Had Schiller read Shakespeare's play? Whether he had or not, the comparison remains instructive; for it allows us to observe the two playwrights dealing with the same kind of subject, and it shows how widely they differ in style and mode of treatment. It is true that the situations, though very similar, are not exactly alike; Philip's jealousy does not, like that of Leontes, flare up spontaneously; it is deliberately aroused by malevolent advisers. This divergence, however, does not in itself account for the fact that the character of jealousy and its manifestations in the two plays are totally unlike. The self-generated jealousy of Leontes is like the sudden outbreak of a virulent disease, a fever in the blood. The victim himself experiences and describes it as something intensely physical:

> I have tremor cordis on me: my heart dances;
> But not for joy; not joy.

> ... and I find it,
> And that to the infection of my brains
> And hardening of my brows.

> Many a thousand on's
> Have the disease, and feel't not.

While the fit is upon him, Leontes is not amenable to reason, incapable of self-control, and forgetful of the elementary decencies of civilized behaviour. In all these respects, he and Philip are poles apart. Though grieved and bitterly resentful, Philip controls his anger with superb dignity; he weighs the evidence, examines the motives of his informants, and decides to take further advice. Where Leontes, obsessed with the physical details of his wife's supposed infidelity, loses his head, Philip is determined to keep his. The language Leontes uses—

> No barricado for a belly: know't;
> It will let in and out the enemy
> With bag and baggage

cannot be imagined on Philip's lips; not merely because this would not suit the style of Schiller's play, nor because Schiller would have shrunk from such directness of utterance (he had used it freely enough in *Die Räuber*!): but because the passion of jealousy, which Shakespeare presents in the raw, is intellectualized in *Don Carlos*. It had been Schiller's professed intention to infuse into Carlos something of Hamlet's soul. Whether intentionally or not, he did the same for Philip; the scenes which show the King's reflective nature in the grip of jealousy reveal a marked family likeness between father and son.

This intellectualizing tendency which seeks to transform the naive into the reflective is seen at work again in Schiller's next play—the play of which Coleridge is reported to have said: "The *Wallenstein* is the greatest of his works; it is not unlike Shakespeare's historical plays—a species by itself." [24] Once again, the influence of Shakespeare is plain to see, and Schiller himself stresses it repeatedly in his correspondence; writing to his friend Körner, for instance (7th April 1797), he states that his study of Shakespeare will have important consequences for his own play, and in a letter to Goethe (28th November 1796) he invokes "the example of Macbeth". It was soon after the completion of *Wallenstein* that he produced his translation of *Macbeth*, and the affinities between the two plays are evident. Both treat the theme of "vaulting ambition, which o'erleaps itself". Their heroes are power-seekers who commit crimes in order to gain their ends, and in both cases their initial scruples are overruled by strong-willed women, whose single-minded determination prevails over the protagonists' infirmity of purpose. In both plays the representatives of the established order close their ranks against the usurper and bring about his downfall. And the temptation which the witches put in Macbeth's way by their "supernatural soliciting" has its counterpart in the favourable conjunction of the stars which Wallenstein interprets as an incitement to treason.

Few would quarrel with Coleridge's assertion that Schiller's play is a great work in its own right; but is it as Shakespearian as he appears to allege? Otto Ludwig (a remarkably perceptive interpreter of Shakespeare, but hopelessly biased where Schiller is concerned) remarks acidly that Schiller's Wallenstein is "neither more nor less than a Hamlet who— Heaven knows how this could have come about—had at one time been something like a Coriolanus", and "who now wants to play Macbeth; not the fierce Scottish thane, though, but one to suit the German ladies".[25] One does not need to agree with the damaging implications of Ludwig's comments to see the differences which underlie the obvious Shakespearian parallels. Both Wallenstein and Coriolanus are proud renegades, great leaders of men who make common cause with the enemy; but while Coriolanus is a born fighter, a man of reckless courage and swift, brutal action, Wallenstein is an intellectual, given to self-analysis, a cautious and calculating schemer. Nor is Wallenstein really akin to Macbeth, for all the similarities of theme and circumstance that link the two plays in the reader's mind. It is true that Macbeth is deeply introspective; but the quality of his introspection is quite different from Wallenstein's, who lacks Macbeth's powerful imagination and his sense of a divine world order which ensures that "in these cases we still have judgment here". Macbeth knows that he cannot "jump the life to come": Wallenstein thinks that he can. As soon as the deed is done, Macbeth's mind is full of scorpions; Wallenstein is under no illusions about the treasonableness of his action, but once he is committed, he seems proof against all scruples and pangs of conscience. Macbeth makes his choice, fully conscious of the retribution that awaits him; Wallenstein does not see that his secret plotting, the "previous dalliance of the fancy with ambitious thoughts ",[26] cannot fail to affect the course of outward events, that the past cannot be sealed off from the present and the future, and that the ambiguity of his former conduct may force his hand under circumstances which, though not of his own choosing, will nevertheless be of his own making.[27]

It would seem, then, that in order to interpret Coleridge's comment aright, the emphasis must be placed at the end, on the words "a species by itself". In other words, what is Shakespearian about *Wallenstein* is not any similarity of character, motivation, or treatment, but the fact that the work is *sui generis*. The more assiduously Schiller studied Shakespeare, the more he endeavoured to learn from the supreme master of his craft, the more he developed his own personal style. Even where he set out to imitate, the result differed from the original, a process which reflects both the distinctive cast of Schiller's mind and the elusiveness of Shakespeare's genius, as his translation of *Macbeth* clearly demonstrates. Taken as a whole, Schiller's version is very effective; in so far as it attempts—not without a measure of success—to recreate the poetry of the original, it is a great advance on the efforts of earlier translators such as Wieland and Eschenburg; and no one could blame a translator for failing to reproduce the peculiarly Shakespearian glory of such lines as

> Will all great Neptune's ocean wash this blood
> Clean from my hand? No, this my hand will rather
> The multitudinous seas incarnadine,
> Making the green one red,

which appear, sadly diluted, as

> Kann der gewässerreiche Meergott selbst
> Mit seinen Fluten allen dieses Blut
> Von meiner Hand abwaschen? Eher färbten
> Sich alle Meere rot von dieser Hand!

What is more to the point than such failure to translate the untranslatable is Schiller's tendency to be more explicit than Shakespeare's text; either in motivation, as in I. 15, where he inserts a lengthy passage of his own to give Lady Macbeth an opportunity of explaining how Malcolm's and Donalbain's claims to the throne may be set aside; or in phrasing, as in III. 2. 55, where the hero's darkly ominous words

> Things bad begun make strong themselves by ill

are expanded into a rhetorical flourish:

> Was blutig anfing, mit Verrat und Mord,
> Das setzt sich nur durch blutge Taten fort!

While some verbal changes of this kind may be unintentional, others, no less revealing, are wholly deliberate. Two essential features of the play, in particular, are transformed beyond recognition. Shakespeare's witches, earthy, primitive, and shadowy embodiments of evil, have in Schiller's version become strangely and self-consciously articulate, explaining their purpose in well-turned and moralizing verses—weird sisters in more ways than one; and Shakespeare's porter of hell-gate has turned into a respectable and eminently sober door-keeper, as incapable of any lurid fantasies as he is of soliciting a tip, who greets the dawn with a pious hymn; "and a charming song, too" (as Quiller-Couch observes), "with the one drawback that it ruins the great dramatic moment of the play".[28]

Few German writers of the eighteenth century were sufficiently versed in English to relish Shakespeare's plays in the original. In the main, Goethe's and Schiller's generation received Shakespeare through the distorting medium of garbled and pedestrian prose translations. The vision which burst upon their view, divinely glorious though it was felt to be, was seen by them through a glass, darkly; and it remained thus blurred until A. W. Schlegel's verse translations appeared.[29] Although at first Schlegel's renderings were criticized in some quarters as being obscure, it was through them that Shakespeare finally came to be accepted as a naturalized classic in Germany. Being remarkably and often daringly close to the English text, both in phrasing and in the handling of the blank verse, they at last showed the German reader a true reflection of the nature of Shakespeare's work. At the same time Schlegel's interpretations of Shakespeare's plays ushered in a new era of Shakespeare scholarship and criticism in Germany. A new prophet had arisen; and looking back upon the Shakespeare cult of the older generation, he might have said, in the words from the address to the Athenians ascribed to St. Paul in Acts xvii. 23[30]: "As I was going round looking at the objects of your worship, I noticed among other things an altar bearing the inscription 'To an Unknown God'. What you worship but do not know—this is what I now proclaim."

NOTES

1. One of Jean Paul's early works casts a strange sidelight on this near-deification of Shakespeare. His "Speech of the dead Christ, proclaiming from the top of the universe that there is no God", a tract against atheism in the shape of an apocalyptic vision of a godless world, which forms an excursus—the first "Flower-Piece"—in the novel *Blumen-Frucht- und Dornenstücke* (1796), had originally been drafted under the title "Dead Shakespeare's lament, addressed to a congregation of the dead in church, that there is no God" (1789/90). Cf. Jean Paul, *Sämtliche Werke*, Section I, Vol. 6 (Weimar, 1928), pp. 247 ff.; and Section II, Vol. 3, pp. 163 ff. It is true that the later version has been expanded somewhat, and given a cosmic setting; but the fact remains that Christ here figures in a role for which Shakespeare had previously been cast.
2. First version, June 1771; final version, 1773; published in *Von deutscher Art und Kunst*.
3. Cf. his letter to J. G. Herder, September 1771; Artemis edition, Vol. 18 (Zurich, 1951), p. 163.
4. *Nathan der Weise*, III, 1, lines 1590 ff.
5. *Hamburgische Dramaturgie*, Section 73.
6. *Dichtung und Wahrheit*, Part III, Book 12.
7. *Ibid*. Part II, Book 7.
8. Iago's famous "Credo" in Verdi's *Otello* is one of the few additions inserted into Shakespeare's text by the composer and by his librettist Boito.
9. F. Gundolf points out an analogous contrast between Karl Moor's monologue in IV. 5 and Hamlet's "To be or not to be" soliloquy. Karl Moor's speech is modelled on Hamlet's; but while Hamlet considers the possible consequences of suicide for himself, the starting-point of his reflections being the concrete situation in which he finds himself involved, Schiller's hero begins with a general philosophical question

about the meaning of human life and man's intimations of immortality:
"But why the burning hunger after happiness, why the ideal of
unattained perfection . . . ?" Cf. Friedrich Gundolf, *Shakespeare und der
deutsche Geist*, 6th edn. (Berlin, 1922), pp. 299 f.

10. Roy Pascal, *Shakespeare in Germany* (Cambridge, 1937), p. 14.
11. For a fuller discussion of this problem, cf. W. Witte, "The Sociological
    Approach to Literature", *Modern Language Review*, XXXVI. 1;
    January 1941.
12. *Biographia Literaria*, chapter xxii, at the end.
13. *Dichtung und Wahrheit*, Part III, Book 15.
14. *Ibid*. Part III, Book 11.
15. 1 Corinthians xv. 10.
16. Cf. *Dichtung und Wahrheit*, Part III, Book 13: "Through my continuous
    interest in Shakespeare's works I had so enlarged my mind that the
    narrow space of the stage and the short time allotted to a performance
    seemed quite inadequate to the treatment of a significant subject."
17. *Ibid*. Part IV, Book 20.
18. Book IV, chapter 13, at the end.
19. A. C. Bradley, *Shakespearean Tragedy*, 2nd edn. (London, 1937), pp. 101
    ff.; J. Dover Wilson, *What Happens in "Hamlet"* (Cambridge, 1935), pp.
    43, 50; A. A. Jack, *Young Hamlet* (Aberdeen, 1950), pp. 7 ff.; Allardyce
    Nicoll, *Studies in Shakespeare* (London, 1931), pp. 41 ff.; T. S. Eliot,
    "Hamlet"; reprinted in *Selected Prose* (Penguin, 1953), p. 104.
20. A. A. Jack, *loc. cit.*, p. 12.
21. Friedrich Gundolf, *loc. cit.* p. 316.
22. Letter to W. F. Reinwald, 14th April 1783.
23. This, of course, does not establish any negative proof. There is no
    reason why Schiller's letters, numerous though they are, should
    contain explicit references to all the plays he had read. Some plays of
    Shakespeare's which he evidently knew—such as *The Comedy of Errors*,
    The Merchant of Venice, *The Tempest*—are mentioned only once in the
    whole corpus of his correspondence; others—such as *Richard II*, the two
    Parts of *Henry IV*, *Henry V*, and the three Parts of *Henry VI*—are referred to
    by implication only.
24. Coleridge's *Table Talk*, 16th February 1833.
25. Otto Ludwig, *Dramatische Studien*: Schiller.
26. *Coleridge's Shakespearean Criticism*, ed. by T. M. Raysor, Vol. I (London,
    1930), p. 68.
27. For a more detailed statement of these points, cf. W. Witte, "Time in
    Wallenstein and *Macbeth*", in *Schiller and Burns and Other Essays* (Oxford,
    1959); W. Witte, edition of *Wallensteins Tod* (Oxford, 1962), pp.
    xxxvii ff.: "*Wallenstein* and Shakespeare."
28. Sir Arthur Quiller-Couch, *Shakespeare's Workmanship* (Cambridge, 1931),
    p. 28.
29. Seventeen plays appeared between 1797 and 1810. The rest were
    translated later (1825-33) by Dorothea Tieck and Count Wolf
    Baudissin.
30. Some classical and New Testament scholars have argued that the
    ascription to St. Paul is unwarrantable; cf. Eduard Norden, *Agnostos
    Theos* (Leipzig and Berlin, 1923), pp. 6, 127 f.

James George

ADDITIONAL MATERIALS
ON THE LIFE OF THOMAS LODGE
BETWEEN 1604 AND 1613

I

The close of the year A.D. 1596 saw a profound change in the life of Thomas Lodge, which falls into two very distinct periods divided at this point.[1] In the earlier, the period of his plays and poems, of *Rosalynde* and his other romances, Lodge, after being a student at Oxford and Lincoln's Inn, had lived a far from satisfactory life as a man about town and man of letters. Then, about the end of 1596 or early in 1597, when he was thirty-nine, he left London for Avignon to study medicine and graduated there as Doctor of Medicine on 13th January 1598.[2] Though he did not cease to write (on graver topics), it is primarily as a practising physician that we hear of him thereafter.

Already in 1596 Lodge had published a devotional book, *Prosopopeia The Teares of the Holy, Blessed, and Sanctified Marie, the Mother of God*, and it is clear that in the second period of his life he had become a Roman Catholic, though at what date is not known.

Anthony à Wood records that he was much frequented for his success in physic "especially by R. Catholics"[3] and a report of 1601 [4] states that certain recusants were resorting to him early in that year for treatment at his house at Lambert Hill (in Queenhithe Ward); it also appears that he accompanied these patients to Spa, where he stayed two or three months, and that at the time he also had a house in Liège. He was back in London in June 1602 [5] and was incorporated M.D. at Oxford in October. During the plague of 1603 he continued to practise in the City, though many another doctor left in the face of the epidemic, and dated his *Treatise of the Plague* from his house in Warwick Lane (in Farringdon Ward Within) on 19th August 1603. On 11th May 1604 he was examined by the Royal College of Physicians for their Licence, but failed (*parum satisfecit*).[6]

Lodge had also married at a date unknown. "There is some evidence", writes Dr. Alice Walker,[7] "that his wife was Jane Aldred, widow of Solomon Aldred. . . . A pedigree in the Vincent Collection shows that

Jane Aldred was the 'doughter of John Fernelay of Rede in com. Herford'."
This identification can be regarded as certain, for in the documents which
I shall cite later Lodge refers to his "brother fferneley".[8] The Parish
Registers of Reed in Hertfordshire mention [9] the birth of five children of
John Farnisley (the name is variously spelt): on 17th October 1543 his
son Walter was born, on 22nd September 1544 his son Samuel, and on
1st September 1546 his daughter Johane, who is no doubt Lodge's future
wife. She was thus a good deal his senior, for he is believed to have been
born in 1558. Nevertheless she survived him. There appears also to
have been another son William whose birth is not mentioned in these
registers.

It is possible to add a good deal of information regarding these
children.

Miss Clare Talbot has recently published from the Yelverton MSS.
in the British Museum a list drawn up by an English agent in
1580 which includes among recusant laymen in Rome "Salomon
Aldred,[10] some tyme a hosier in Birchine Lane in London, he married
the sister of Wm Ferneslye & sent to Rome by Walter Fernesley who
gave to them 300 crownes for to heare [11] ther charges".[12] Aldred is
said to have been in receipt of a pension of 10 crowns a month from
the Pope.

The same list also describes two recusants "at Liones in France". The
entry is as follows:

> Walter Ferneslye—merchant, he hath maried a French woman. His
> house a great harbour for all papists that pass by him. He sent Sallamon
> Aldred who married his sister to Rome & gave unto his said brother and
> sister 300 crownes of golde to bear the (sic) charges he hath also a partner
> called Mr Hanford dwellinge at the Stokes to whom I hath demeth (sic),
> doth send letters to (sic) delivered to sundry persons in London and also in
> other places of the Realme and likewise the said Hanford doth send unto
> him, which doth send abroad.
>
> Samuell Fernesley—merchant, brother to the said Walter, he hath bene
> the laste yere at Jerusalem for devocions sake & hath brought from there
> Agnus Deies & graynes & earth of the Sepuckur & doth disperse them
> abroade to sundry persons.[13]

The final section of the list gives "the names of them that are in
England", including "William Fernesly, dwellinge at Royston, he hath a
howse at Barkway [14] and also in the Eyle of Elye & in divers other
places".[15]

The author lodged with Solomon Aldred in Rome in July and August
1579,[16] so that his information seems well-founded.

Lodge's "brother fferneley" was, I believe, Walter, who was a
successful merchant, described as living at Lyons "in good state" in
October 1601 [17] and paying Fr. Robert Persons £50 a year for the
maintenance of his son.[18] He was still living at Lyons in September 1603.[19]
This son was Andrew Fernesley who at the age of 14½ was admitted to the
English College at Rome in April 1600. The following passage from his

Responsum [20] is worth quoting for the picture it gives of the Ferneley family
and its spirit:

> Pater ex Anglia, mater ex Sabaudia oriundi sunt. Pater quam a multo
> tempore exercuerat mercaturam deposuit, neque iam ullam artem factitat.
> Nullos habeo fratres, sorores totidem: unicam tamen habui, quae mensem
> nata a seculo migravit. Cognatum paterno nomine in Anglia habeo unicum,
> Iurisconsultum scilicet, cuius de fide asserere nil ausim: ipse enim nuper
> cum Lugdunum venisset haereticus, infirmus in Angliam catholicus brevi
> ducturus uxorem reversus est: Caeteros autem Dei gratia sive affines sive
> consanguineos Catholicos habeo.

Mrs. Lodge also appears to have been a devout Catholic.

II

With so much of introduction I turn to the next references which occur
to Thomas Lodge himself.

In February 1604/5[21] "Thomas Lodge nuper de paroch' ecclesie
Christi in warda de Farringdon infra [22] in medicinis doctor" was indicted
with four others, including Hugh Holland,[23] because "they did not
repayre" to their parish churches or any other church during the month
commencing the 10th January but "have forborne the same". Again on
3rd January 1605/6 Lodge (who is described as before) was indicted in
the same terms for failing to attend any Church during the three months
commencing on 5th October 1605.[24] Among the eighteen persons now
indicted with him were "Beniaminus Johnson", generosus (of Black-
friars), Martin Pierson (of St. Olave's, Silver Street, "musician") and
Edmund Bolton, generosus (of St. Thomas the Apostle in Vintry Ward).
On each occasion a true bill was found, and those indicted were "pro-
claimed in accordance with the Statute". It appears that Lodge did
nothing to deny the charge. The consequence, on formal conviction at the
next Session, was that Lodge became liable to a penalty of £20 for each
month in which he did not attend an Anglican Church, but there is no
sign that the authorities did anything to enforce this penalty.[25]

Dr. Alice Walker suggested [26] that the future Bishop Joseph Hall may
have met Lodge in Brussels in April or May 1605, when he was on his way to
Spa with Sir Edmund Bacon. Hall states [27] that when Sir Edmund Bacon and
he arrived in Brussels the English Ambassador, the Earl of Hertford, "had
newly sat down" there before them. Hertford landed at Dunkirk on 20th
April; he reached Brussels on the 27th and stayed there twelve days.[28]
The earlier of the two indictments mentioned is therefore not inconsistent
with the conjecture that the gentleman Hall met in Brussels ("who, having
run himself out of breath in the inns of court, had forsaken his country, and
therewith his religion; and was turned both bigot and physician, residing

now in Brussels") [29] was Lodge. If, however, Lodge was this gentleman he will have returned to England by the following October, since it is hardly likely that he could have been indicted again, if he had remained abroad.

It is certain that Lodge left England after the second of the indictments to which I have referred for there is in existence an intercepted letter [30] dated 9th March 1605/6 addressed to him from London by a recusant William Jenison [31] who says "I cannot but congratulate your departure hence to live in such contentment as their I heare you doe". He had gone again to the Spanish Netherlands (leaving his wife in England for the time being), and as this was not the first letter Jenison had written him, it can be concluded that he left quite soon after the second indictment; the indications are that he left quite hurriedly. As Professor Sisson, who dwells on Lodge's unthriftiness and financial difficulties, has suspected that in the period 1601 to 1603 he had not been making a success of his profession, [32] it should perhaps be pointed out that this letter shows that Lodge had invested at least £50 in a voyage set out by the Muscovy Company (of which his father had once been Governor) in 1604. In 1606, Mrs. Lodge was able to agree on her husband's behalf that his investment should remain in the hands of the Company as part of the stock to finance a further voyage. It would have been possible for her to "take out his stock and forbeare to be anie further adventurer", and, when her husband had taken refuge in the Netherlands, she might have been expected to do so, but she did not. Indeed Jenison clearly thought that Lodge would continue to put money into these ventures. [33]

III

Of Lodge's life during the next five years his biographers have nothing to say. "Lodge was not able to look homeward for some five years, as far as is known" wrote Paradise, [34] adding that when he was admitted to the College of Physicians in March 1610, it was probably *in absentia*. Walker says that "probably for the whole of this period (1606-11) Lodge was out of England". [35] Less cautiously Sisson [36] resumed his account of Lodge with the words "Lodge was allowed to return early in 1611". Tenney [37] and Ryan, the latest writer on Lodge's life, [38] have nothing to add.

There is, however, quite a lot of material towards filling in this five-year gap, and first a document from the Royal Archives in Brussels, [39] which has been generously communicated to me by the Curator, Mademoiselle L. Van Meerbeeck, and may be translated [40] as follows:

> Know that Dr. Thomas Lodgie, former doctor of the infantry regiment under Colonel Count Thomas de Arondel, has informed us of his services and of the fact that, the said regiment and its officer-staff having been

disbanded, he has been left without pay. He has asked us to order that he be put on the pay-list so that he can continue to serve the better in the future [;] and we in consideration of the aforesaid have decided to do so, and hereby assign him 20 escudos pay per month, he serving as doctor in the Irish infantry regiment of Colonel Henry O'Neill; wherefore etc. . . . Dated Brussels 30 June 1606, from [41] when the said infantry regiment was disbanded.

Sir Thomas Arundel (a Count of the Holy Roman Empire since 1595), who was created Baron Arundel of Wardour in the summer of 1605, had been permitted to raise a regiment of Englishmen for service with the Spaniards in the Netherlands. From the formation of the regiment in August it seems to have been bedevilled with discords, culminating in a mutiny after which it was "reformed". Arundel claimed that his difficulties were due to the efforts of the Jesuit party among the English refugees in Flanders (headed by such men as Hugh Owen) to dominate the regiment. "The Jesuited sort", he asserted, "held it as an undoubted maxim that no man is fit to command either regiment or company that professes a dutiful respect to the Crown of England"; he, on the other hand, remained a loyal Englishman and "stiffly opposed himself" to them, "permitting none (as near as I could) to bear office in the regiment that depended of them".[42] The facts that Lodge secured an appointment from Arundel and that when the regiment broke up he was not retained, suggest that his attitude in these matters was similar to his Colonel's; indeed Lodge said in 1609 [43] that "his heart is and hath always been free from intending anything against either Prince or Country".

Mademoiselle Van Meerbeeck, the acknowledged authority in Belgium on the history of the military hospitals there during the Spanish period, informs me that she knows of no other reference to Lodge in the archives.

Previous biographers [44] have, however, drawn attention to the fact that in a late work, *The Poore Mans Talentt*,[45] Lodge gives a remedy "which I have often tried in the Roiall Hospitall att Macklin Vppon Souldiers that growe lame by coulde". Though Mademoiselle Van Meerbeeck tells me that she does not think that Lodge was on the staff of the Hospital, the reference seems to be to this period of Lodge's life, for in a letter of 2nd July 1609 [46] he speaks of "some of our officers in the hospital".

There is unfortunately some doubt about the date of the next pieces of information regarding Lodge. In 1936 the second volume of a *Calendar of the Marquess of Downshire's Manuscripts* was issued by The Historical Manuscripts Commission. The papers calendared are the correspondence of William Trumbull, who served as secretary to Sir Thomas Edmondes while he was Ambassador at Brussels and, when Edmondes was recalled in 1609, remained there as the English representative (though with the title not of Ambassador but of Agent). This volume contains no less than eight letters from Lodge to Trumbull which have not previously been noticed. Of these I take first two letters dated by Lodge 13th April 1607 [47] and 23rd April 1607.[48] They are, however, endorsed as of the same dates in 1608. The editor of the *Calendar*, A. B. Hinds, believes [49] that the endorsements are wrong, but since they were made by the methodical Trumbull, they should, I believe, be regarded as right.[50] The letters were certainly addressed to Trumbull in Brussels, and the editor infers that at the time of writing Lodge was again in London and indeed had recently arrived there from the Netherlands. This, however, by no means necessarily follows. It seems just as possible that when he wrote them, Lodge was at some other place in the Netherlands, and, indeed much more likely since, as far as is known, he still held a commission in the Archduke's forces.[51] Another letter,[52] which is dated by Lodge 25th February 1609, must also be considered here, for it is likewise endorsed by Trumbull "25th February 1608". Unfortunately the contents of the letter do not provide any very clear indication of its true date, but what evidence there is favours the year 1608. Indeed it is, I believe, the first letter of this series.

"It is noteworthy", writes the editor,[53] "that in most of his letters Lodge calls Trumbull his son and writes as if he had married Trumbull's mother", leaving the matter at that. The use of the word "son" in this sense was, however, no more than an expression of affection.[54] Sir John Throckmorton, Deputy Governor of Flushing, also addressed Trumbull as "son"[55]; he also signed himself "your adopted father". [56] Indeed in a later letter to Trumbull Lodge himself wrote "I am not in effect (i.e. in reality) your father".[57] It is perhaps more unusual that in writing to Trumbull he should refer to his wife as "your mother".[58]

Early in 1608 then we find Lodge still in the Netherlands (where he had now been joined by his wife) on terms of affectionate intimacy with Sir Thomas Edmondes's household. Trumbull had been consistently helpful. In the letter of 25th February Lodge speaks of the "great dejection and amasedness my present misfortune hath brought me into, yea to be plain with you it hath wellnigh made myself forget myself" (he had indeed forgotten also to send two prescriptions for which he had been asked). He asked Trumbull to have a letter transmitted to a Mr. Gent [59]; what this contained does not appear, but Lodge considered it very important. The letters of April again speak of the misfortunes weighing Lodge and his wife down and go on to deal with two particular points. They had just heard that Mrs. Lodge's daughter, Lady Cooke,[60] was dangerously ill and perhaps already dead; they are anxious to have news of her, and again there was a letter to be sent to Mr. Gent asking for information. Lodge also asked whether, if the Ambassador was having a consignment of goods sent over to him from England, there was any chance that he could arrange to have "his books" sent over with them, though he subsequently abandoned this idea. Apparently he had left at least part [61] of his library behind when he left England in 1606. A letter dated 6th July 1608 [62] written to Trumbull in London by John Beaulieu says that Trumbull had been sent a letter by "Mrs. Lodge", asking him to bring back a bloodhound. This shows that Mrs. Lodge visited England in the summer of

1608, and it may perhaps be conjectured that Lady Cooke survived her "desperate sickness" and that her mother had gone home to be with her.

The next five letters date from 1609 and concern what was, no doubt, the most important event in this period of Lodge's life. The earliest [63] is dated 20th April 1609, and deals with Lodge's "resolution for England".

The Twelve Years' Truce between Spain and the United Provinces had been concluded in March and in a letter [64] from Brussels dated 11th April Sir Thomas Edmondes had written:

> It is expected that the next work they will here go in hand withal will be the discharging of the greatest part of their men of war; but therein they do first attend the order of Spain, as also for means to satisfy them upon their dismission what is owing them, which will be a thing of no small difficulty to perform, by reason of the present necessities of Spain.

Lodge was still, so far as is known, medical officer to a regiment in the pay of Spain and these developments had obliged him to consider what course he should now take. He had consulted Trumbull on the advisability of returning to England, and Trumbull had replied approving the idea but advising Lodge that he must be careful to ensure that he would not be liable to prosecutions in England and that he could achieve his "dispatch in every respect in this place", which refers primarily to the arrears of salary which Lodge was due, what (like other officers) Lodge called his *rematto*. Lodge agreed, remarking: "I know and foresee the delay and procrastination of the court and commanders in these parts, especially for money matters." This matter of the *rematto* recurs again and again in his subsequent correspondence. In January 1617 Lodge and another were permitted to go "to the Archdukes' country" for five months [65] "to recover such debtes as are due to them there"—in Lodge's case, I have no doubt, the *rematto*; and indeed I know no evidence that when he died in 1625 he had been paid in full.

Lodge then turns to the matter of freedom from prosecution in England. He fears he may have been misrepresented while a refugee abroad for "there is a sort of vermin that skulketh about; some call them necessary evils, others intelligencers, who having great men's ears chained to their tongue, do oftentimes breathe into them more poisonous surmises by their misreports than of their own wisdom they should admit or conscience allow of". He asks Trumbull to counteract any such reports. He aims at obtaining "no less favour than many others of my rank have in England that under some counsellors' hands are defensed from troubles either in life or fortune", and asks Trumbull to do his uttermost to achieve this for him. He is able to be more specific, for he adds "There is one Spiller [66] that in this sort (upon some gratuity) yieldeth them security, by whom you may endeavour in my behalf"—nor was Trumbull himself to go unrecompensed.

Though, when Lodge wrote, Trumbull had already left for London,[67] he clearly thought his letter would arrive before he went. He would, he says, have come to say goodbye in person "but Plutus the churl denied me a viaticum". With this letter therefore he took leave of him "as an old

Genouais did of me of the noble House of the Adorni when after many kind offices done unto him on Mr. Caundishes expedition I was to depart and ready to set sail: *Vale*, said he, *mi fili, Deus te salvum reducat in domum tuam*".[68]

Lodge's next letter is dated the 2nd July 1609.[69] Trumbull is back in Brussels, and Lodge is anxious to know whether he has contrived to "work my protection". However, even if he has not succeeded, Lodge means to return to England, making arrangements for the collection of his *rematto* in his absence. He was concerned about paying off debts to an English merchant in Antwerp (which came to £54) before he left; he does not seem to have the money to do so. He asks if Trumbull knows "any means for the sauf convoy of my trunks" to England. Ten days later an excited letter [70] follows. Once again there is a letter to be forwarded as soon as possible to Mr. Gent, and Trumbull is asked to "procure me an effectual certificate from mine honourable Lord" (Sir T. Edmondes) "whereby he" (Mr. Gent) "may effectuate my freedom of practice before my coming into England". It seems that during his visit to England Trumbull had found a "friend" who was willing to procure Lodge a "dispensation from the Council". "Write to him" (Mr. Gent) urges Lodge, "and direct him, address him to your friend, animate your friend in my behalf". Lodge was particularly anxious that the dispensation should be secured before he reached England, saying cryptically "in my absence that thing may be wrought which my presence may make difficult by reason of the oppositions I told you of"—what these may have been does not appear.

During his visit to England Trumbull had been charged with arranging for the return of Sir Thomas Edmondes also, and already at the beginning of August the Ambassador writes [71] that he is "preparing to dislodge from hence". He appears to have reached London early in September. Exactly when Lodge returned cannot be said, but we have a letter [72] from him to Trumbull dated 21st September 1609 in which he writes "both I and your Mother salute you. . . . We are now safe arrived in London, I thank God, and as yet secured from any disaster."

IV

The words "as yet secured from any disaster" imply, I think, that in the event Lodge had returned to England without his "dispensation from the Council" having been previously "dispatched",[73] and this would explain what he goes on to say. "My Lord", he writes, "continueth his good affection, and we hope upon opportunity to reap the fruits thereof. In the meanwhile if your good commend to some your honest and familiar friends in Court may sted us in the suit we prosecute, make me known to him, I pray you, by a letter that I may have recourse unto him upon occasion". The background of Lodge's life for about the next eighteen months in thus set.

We may turn for a time, however, to lighter themes. In the same letter Lodge tells Trumbull that he had sent him, as he had promised, "the *Wars of the Jews* in French" [74] and "the *Comparison of the States of Christendom* in a manuscript which I pray keep seriously for I esteem it". He had indeed handed them over to Beaulieu for transmission, but "the book and a roll" were not sent on to Trumbull till November.[75]

Another letter to Trumbull dated 22nd November 1609, is also preserved [76]—a rather ponderous statement on how a student of political history should organize his reading, a subject on which Trumbull had apparently asked Lodge's advice. "Thus much touching that", writes Lodge, and continues with some items of current news. Some of the incidental statements are interesting. Acknowledging that Trumbull is a busy man, Lodge can add "tho' now my business likewise be important". "I live not in the eye of the world, traffic not with men of State, my court is my study, my courtisans [77] my books." It was perhaps with a very personal interest that Lodge recorded that "A gentleman of great reverence hath lately been searched, and two priests found in his house and his goods confiscate: yet hath his Majesty's mercy dispensed with all for 1,000 marks". Referring inevitably to his *rematto* he "would be glad to have an order for money, for believe me, Son, I am engaged and have spent 200 l. on my house". Clearly, throughout his exile he had retained ownership of a house (perhaps the house in Warwick Lane) which after four years was in need of extensive repair. And to end—"a patient calls away, my candle is now put out". One sees a well-frequented doctor, who on a winter's evening has used a lull in the demands on his professional services to retire to his study and write to a friend, suddenly interrupted by yet another professional call. In his *Troia Brittanica* (1609) Thomas Heywood wrote:

"As famous Butler, Pady, Turner, Poe,
Atkinson, Lyster, Lodge, who still suruiue.
Besides these English Gallens. . . .

This passage has not been without its difficulties for Lodge's previous biographers, but can now be seen as evidence that on his return Lodge quickly re-established his popularity as a physician.

In March 1610 Lodge was admitted to the College of Physicians, and Professor Sisson has found that in November 1610 he borrowed £100 from his brother Nicholas [78]—possibly to pay off the bills on the house-repairs. We next hear of him on 17th January 1610/11, the date of a letter [79]—already well-known—to Sir Thomas Edmondes, now Ambassador in Paris, having arrived there in June 1610. Sisson writes [80] that in this letter Lodge "expressed his thanks to Edmondes for his help in bringing about this repatriation", but this, I believe, was not his real reason for writing. Lodge's words "by whose means I have not only reposs[ess]ed my

Country, but my peace and quietness in the same" mean, I believe, that Lodge now knew that through Edmondes's good offices he would receive a "dispensation from the Council", and indeed on 28th January 1610/11 the Privy Council wrote [81] to the Clerk of the Peace for Middlesex and the Town Clerk of the City of London, directing them "if any Endictment be alreadie or shalbe hereafter preferred against Thomas Lodge d^r of Phisicke for his recusancie to detain it in their hands" and refer to the Council for orders. This, it seems clear from the letter, was the outcome of steps taken by Edmondes in his behalf before he left for Paris, for Lodge writes "Now find I your worthines even in your absence, because your Honour so nobly prevented my dangers by your providence at your being heare". It was to thank Edmondes for his part in securing this order that Lodge wrote.

The *Calendar* of Trumbull's papers contains one further letter from Lodge dated 7th October 1613.[82] It is a letter of sententious advice and only the opening sentence need concern us, in which Lodge writes "I hope you will impute my silence to my long absence from London". In September 1612 his brother Nicholas had died at Rolleston, near Newark, and we know [83] that thereafter Lodge went down there to take possession of the estate which now passed to him. How long he stayed at Rolleston on this occasion does not appear, but it would seem to be to this visit that Lodge is referring.

V

This additional material permits us, I think, to revise the opinions which previous biographers have expressed regarding Lodge as a man. Men do not appear at their best in their litigation and this can hardly have been more true of any than of the Elizabethans and Jacobeans; it is Lodge's misfortune that the great bulk of the information hitherto available regarding him has been unearthed from the records of the litigation in which he was involved. To this his letters, in their context, happily provide a corrective. His recollections of his days in Santos in 1591 show us a gentleman-volunteer who in the midst of an attack on the town took pains to befriend an elderly Italian gentleman who might otherwise have fared badly at the hands of the crews of the English ships. The same gift of sympathy appears in his concern for his step-daughter, Lady Cooke. Of the period when he was a refugee in the Netherlands it has been said [84] that "he seems to have had no permanent place of abode". It is hard to believe this of a married man who has his wife with him and he certainly had a succession of posts; it would seem clear from the correspondence that he was latterly well established at Malines; it appears also that he never abandoned his house in London. A convinced Catholic, he secured an appointment in Lord Arundel's regiment, but was not retained when extremists, animated by anti-English feeling above all else, assumed control; essentially Lodge was a loyal Englishman—were this not so, he could not have maintained his happy relations with the English Ambassador in Brussels, his secretaries, and his household, and feel that he could count on their help—and help him they did. "He arrived back in England", writes Professor Sisson [85] "in need of money, as ever, and alternating from poverty to indebtedness or both." Here surely some correction is necessary and possible. Lack of ready money was a common feature of Jacobean life, from which the refugees suffered more than most, and Spain was notoriously a bad paymaster. It is certain that when Lodge left the Netherlands his pay was in arrears—and probably heavily in arrears. Many of the exiles had little to hope for and must have laboured under a constant sense of frustration, but, though he could complain of his misfortune, Lodge seems to have remained remarkably unsoured, which should perhaps be attributed to his family life and friendships, to his love of books and his devotion to the practice of medicine.

"Spendthrift or improvident to the end, there is never any sign even in his riper years of a settled course of life", writes Professor Sisson.[86] The circumstances of his life in Flanders gave Lodge little chance of being a spendthrift, though improvident he may have been. Certainly the evidence produced here indicates that his pursuit of medicine was a settled course of life.

Professor Sisson [87] finds it the dominant note of the whole of Lodge's life, that he was "an incurably assertive individualist vindicating self-will and private opinion against all the forces of environment". One sees nothing of this in the material here produced.

Lodge once said he might appear [88] "a patron (i.e. pattern) of inconsideration", by which he meant that he might appear negligent of his obligations, and dilatory in the performance of what he had undertaken to do. He was, I think, unmethodical and had never, I suspect, reached a correct adjustment to life as it must be lived. There is a great deal that is unpleasant in the picture we must form of Lodge, but much of it, I think, can be explained as due to the determined efforts of a clever man to remedy the consequences of previous failure to realize the results which neglect of his affairs would have. Such a man, confronted with a situation which he must endeavour to retrieve, can be expected to show the utmost of persistence and to use his ingenuity to the full.

The picture of Mrs. Lodge which here emerges is also new—a devout and practical woman, no longer young, who inspired affection in those she knew, even though not of her own faith, and gave them affection too. There seems no reason to doubt that, despite the disparity in their ages, Lodge and his wife were happily married, though the years covered by this survey were for them mostly years of difficulty and frustration.

Of the letters given in the *Calendar of the Downshire Manuscripts* the editor wrote[89]: "These throw some light, though not a great deal, upon an obscure portion of Lodge's career." This, I venture to suggest, is too modest an estimate and I would claim that they and the other material here produced make a substantial addition to the sources available for a biography of Lodge.

NOTES

1. Alice Walker, *The Life of Thomas Lodge*, R.E.S., Vol. IX (1933), p. 432.
2. Walker, R.E.S., Vol. X (1934), p. 46.
3. *Athenae Oxonienses* (ed. Bliss), II, 382, quoted by N. B. Paradise: *Thomas Lodge, The History of an Elizabethan* (New Haven: Yale U.P., 1931), p. 51.
4. H.M.C., *Salisbury*, Vol. XI, pp. 356-7, quoted by Paradise, *op. cit.* p. 54.
5. Walker, *op. cit.* p. 47.
6. E. A. Tenney, *Thomas Lodge* (Ithaca: Cornell U.P., 1935), p. 171, n. 1.
7. R.E.S., Vol. X (1934), p. 52.
8. H. M. C., *Downshire*, Vol. II, p. 190.
9. I am indebted for this information to Mr. P. Walne, County Archivist of Hertfordshire, who very kindly examined the registers for me. The entries occur in Vol. I.
10. For Solomon Aldred see Fr. Leo Hicks, S.J., "An Elizabethan Propagandist: The Career of Solomon Aldred", in *The Month*, May-June 1945, pp. 181 ff.
11. This should presumably be "beare".
12. *Recusant Records*, ed. Clare Talbot (Publications of the Catholic Record Society, Vol. LIII) (1961), p. 196. I am grateful to the Council of the Society for permission to reproduce this and the other passages given below, and to make use of others of their publications.
13. *Ibid.* p. 201.
14. Reed adjoins Royston and Barkway. The parishes of Reed and Barkway were united in 1800 (V.C.H., *Hertfordshire*, Vol. III, p. 253).
15. *Op. cit.* p. 211.
16. *Ibid.* pp. 214, 222.
17. Foley, *Records of the English Province of the Society of Jesus* (London, 1880), Vol. VI, p. 734.
18. *Cal. State Papers Domestic, Addenda 1580-1625*, p. 413.
19. *The Liber Ruber of the English College, Rome*, ed. Rev. W. Kelly (Publications of the Catholic Record Society, Vol. XXXVII) (1940), p. 118.
20. *The English College at Rome: Responsa, Part I*, ed. A. Kenny (Publications of the Catholic Record Society, Vol. LIV) (1962), p. 66.
21. *London Sessions Records, 1605-1685*, ed. Dom Hugh Bowler, O.S.B. (Publications of the Catholic Record Society, Vol. XXXIV) (1934), p. 3.
22. This confirms Professor Paradise's statement (*op. cit.* p. 54) that Lodge moved from Lambert Hill to Warwick Lane and not, as Wood had said, vice versa.
23. The author of a sonnet prefixed to the First Folio.
24. Bowler, *op. cit.* p. 7. See also Jonson, *Works*, ed. Herford and Simpson, Vol. XI, pp. 579-80. These two indictments are noticed in the brief biography of Lodge given in L. I. Guiney, "Recusant Poets" (London and New York, 1938), p. 233.

25. Bowler, *op. cit.* pp. xliii, xlv.

26. R.E.S., Vol. X (1934), pp. 47-49.

27. Joseph Hall, *Works* (ed. 1837), Vol. I, p. xx.

28. See G. B. Harrison, *A Jacobean Journal* (London, 1941), p. 205, citing Stow's *Annales*.

29. Hall, *loc. cit.* It is perhaps worth noting that Sir Edmund Bacon's grandmother (the wife of Queen Elizabeth's Lord Keeper) was born Jane Fernely. I have, however, been unable to trace any connection with the Ferneleys of Reed. Is it possible that Lodge made a point of seeing Sir Edmund when he was in Brussels because of some distant family connection with his wife, and that this helped to make Lodge's attentions unwelcome?

30. S. P. Dom. Jac. I, 19/26; *C.S.P. Dom. 1603-1610*, p. 298. Reprinted by Gosse in *The Complete Works of Thomas Lodge* (Hunterian Club, 1883), Vol. I, pp. 41-43, Paradise, *op. cit.* pp. 55-56, Tenney, *op. cit.* pp. 175-6.

31. On Jenison see Anne C. M. Forster, *A Durham Family: Jenisons of Walworth*, in *Biographical Studies* (now *Recusant History*) Vol. III, pp. 2-15. Lodge had given evidence for him in May 1604 (C. J. Sisson in *Thomas Lodge and other Elizabethans* (Cambridge, Mass., 1933), pp. 108-9).

32. Sisson, *op. cit.* pp. 109-10.

33. Cf. Tenney, *op. cit.* p. 176, n. 1. See also T. S. Willan, *The Early History of the Russia Company* (Manchester U.P., 1956), pp. 212-16.

34. Paradise, *op. cit.* p. 56; later Paradise treats 1611 as the year of Lodge's return (*ibid.* p. 58). In a later article of 1935 (Yale Journal of Medicine and Biology, vii (1934-5), p. 509) Paradise cites a statement that Lodge passed the examination at the Royal College of Physicians in 1609. This seems, however, to relate to the same occasion as his admission as a Licentiate on 9th March, 1609/10.

35. R.E.S., Vol. X, p. 47; on p. 49 Dr. Walker writes "On his return from exile early in 1611".

36. Sisson, *op. cit.* p. 110.

37. See Tenney, *op. cit.* pp. 176-7. There is no substance in his surmise that Lodge may have spent part of the time in France and may have practised in Paris. This seems to be no more than an unjustified inference from the fact that when Lodge wrote a letter of thanks to Sir Thomas Edmondes in January 1610/11 he addressed him as Ambassador in Paris.

38. P. M. Ryan, *Thomas Lodge, Gentleman* (Hamden, The Shoe String Press, 1958).

39. *Archives générales du Royaume à Bruxelles; Secrétairerie d'Etat et de Guerre, Registre aux ordres de l'armée espagnole des Pays-Bas*, no. 23, fo. 356, v°.

40. I am obliged for this translation to Mr. T. E. May, Lecturer in Spanish in the University of Aberdeen. The original reads:

"Alberto etc.
   Don Francesco, etc.
   Saved que el Doctor Thomas Lodgie, medico que le ha sido del tercio de infanteria Inglesa conque servia el coronel conde Thomas de Arondel, nos ha representado sus servicios y que per haverse reformado el dicho tercio y los officialos mayores del, ha quedado sin sueldo. Supplicado nos se le mandasemos senalar paraque adelante pueda continuar sus servicios con mas comodidad y nos teniendo consideracion a lo sobredicho hemos tenido por bien de señalar le como per tenor de la presente le señalamos veynte scudos de sueldo al mes, serviendo de medico en el tercio de infanteria Irlandesa de coronel Don Enrique O'Neill; Por tanto, etc. . . . , Data en Bruselas, 30 de Junio 1606 para desde que se reformo el dicho tercio."

The document is an order directed to the Contador of the Army, Don Francesco Vaca. It appears that Spinola, the general commanding the Spanish forces, appointed a "Colonel Francisco" to command the English Regiment after Arundel's removal (H.M.C., *Salisbury*, Vol. XVIII, pp. 208-22) (July 1606).

41. The word is illegible in the original, but there can be no doubt that "para" is correct.

42. H.M.C., *Salisbury*, Vol. XVIII, p. 376 (cf. *ibid*. p. 31).

43. H.M.C., *Downshire*, Vol. II, p. 93.

44. Paradise, *op. cit.* p. 52; Walker, R.E.S., Vol. X, p. 47; Tenney, *op. cit.* p. 176.

45. *Op. cit.* p. 83, in *Works* (ed. Gosse, Hunterian Club), Vol. IV.

46. H.M.C., *Downshire*, Vol. II, p. 113.

47. *Ibid.* pp. 24-5.

48. *Ibid.* p. 94.

49. *Ibid.* p. xix.

50. For a similar error by a letter-writer, cf. the note at H.M.C., *D'Lisle & Dudley*, Vol. V, p. 104:
"There can be no doubt that the date of this letter should be 5th of April 1613, and that the date it bears 5th of April 1612 is simply due to a slip of Throckmorton's" (i.e the writer's).

51. Indeed the text itself shows this. In the second letter Lodge says that Trumbull's "sudden departure" will prevent Lodge from seeing him before he leaves, and goes on to ask him to see Mr. Gent "upon his arrival in England". From this it seems to follow that Lodge was in the Netherlands and not in London. The two letters follow each other in very close sequence for Trumbull is to ask Mr. Gent to answer a letter from Mrs. Lodge quickly, which seems to be the letter which Lodge had asked Trumbull on 13th April to forward.
   In a letter dated 6th May 1607 (H.M.C., *Downshire*, Vol. II, p. 25) Jean Beaulieu writing to Trumbull, his fellow-secretary, in London, acknowledges a letter from him dated 22nd April. In 1607, therefore, Trumbull must have left Brussels before 23rd April, and it follows that these two letters were not written in that year.

52. H.M.C., *Downshire*, Vol. II, pp. 249-50.

53. *Ibid.* p. xix.

54. Cf. D. Nicholas *Mr Secretary Nicholas* (London, The Bodley Head, 1955), 275: "There has been some confusion among editors as to who Susan" (daughter of Sir Edward Nicholas) "did marry. They have been led astray by the fact that both Lord Newburgh and Middleton write to Edward as father. This was purely a term of affection." This as late as 1655.

55. H.M.C., *Downshire*, Vol. IV, pp. 42, 408, 420. Others did so too.

56. *Ibid.* p. 127.

57. *Ibid.* p. 215.

58. H.M.C., *Downshire*, Vol. II, p. 93.

59. Perhaps the William Gent who was a member of John Chamberlain's circle of friends.

60. It is known that Mrs. Lodge had a daughter Agnes by her first marriage (Walker, R.E.S., Vol. X, p. 52) and she is presumably the person referred to. I have not been able to identify her husband.

61. H.M.C., *Downshire*, Vol. II, p. 94 "that little remainder".

62. *Ibid.* p. 66.

63. *Ibid.* pp. 92-94.

64. E. Lodge, *Illustrations* (1838), Vol. III, p. 253.

65. *A.P.C.*, ed. Dasent, *1616-1617*, p. 116. Tenney, who suggests that Lodge may have been "involved in Papal affairs", asks (*op. cit.* p. 173) "who is to say if the object of the 1617 journey was primarily the collection of debts?" The conjecture regarding Lodge's motives implicit in this question is, I consider, totally unfounded.

66. This appears to be Henry Spiller, Attorney of the Exchequer (H.M.C., *Salisbury*, Vol. XVIII, pp. 10, 398). He was responsible for the realization of dues from recusants. His brother was reported to be a priest (*ibid.* p. 10) and other members of his family to be Roman Catholics. (Compare also the petition printed by Talbot at *Recusant Records*, p. 163.)

67. H.M.C., *Downshire*, Vol. II, p. 90. A warrant dated 24th April 1609 for £10 in Trumbull's favour for bringing letters from Brussels is entered in the Treasurer of the Chamber's Accounts (P.R.O., Deposited Accounts (Audit Office), A.O.1/389/46).

68. An interesting reference to Lodge's experiences at Santos in Brazil in 1591-92. In 1935 Paradise (Yale Journal of Biology and Medicine, vii, p. 501) remarked of Lodge's voyage with Cavendish: "Lodge seems to show no sign of his experience, except that he says that he found the story of *A Margarite of America* at Santos." This, it can now be said, was not so. In 1582 Captain Edward Fenton met "one Josef Adorno a Jenawain borne" (Hakluyt calls him "Joffo Dore") off Santos. He owned a sugar plantation and refinery near by. His daughter had married an English merchant, John Whithall, who had initiated the sugar trade between Brazil and London. (E. G. R. Taylor, *The Troublesome Voyage of Captain Edward Fenton* (London, Hakluyt Society, 1959), p. 126.) This was no doubt the man of whom Lodge writes. In 1582 Whithall was still at Santos, but had perhaps died by 1591, which would explain why it fell to Lodge to befriend his father-in-law. Sisson believes that Lodge returned to England in the *Dainty* which had obtained a cargo of sugar, in which Lodge may have had a financial interest (*op. cit.* p. 108). His connection with Adorno could have made him instrumental in securing this cargo.

69. H.M.C., *Downshire*, Vol. II, pp. 112-13.

70. *Ibid.* pp. 114-15.

71. *Ibid.* p. 115.

72. *Ibid.* p. 140.

73. It may, I think, be conjectured that Lodge did so, in order to travel with Sir Thomas Edmondes's household.

74. In 1602 Lodge had published *The Lamentable and Tragicall Historie of the Wars and vtter rvine of the Iewes. Comprised in seven Bookes by Flavius Iosephus, the Sonne of Matthias. And newly translated out of the Latin, and French into English by Tho. Lodge, D.M.P.* (See Miscellaneous Pieces in *Works* (ed. Hunterian Club), Vol. IV, p. 27). This was, perhaps, the French translation he had used.

75. H.M.C., *Downshire*, Vol. II, pp. 139, 182.

76. *Ibid.* pp. 189-90.

77. I.e. "courtiers" (O.E.D., s.v., sb.1).

78. Sisson, *op. cit.* p. 110.

79. B.M., Stowe MSS, 171, fo. 352. Printed in *Works* (ed. Hunterian Club), Vol. IV, Miscellaneous Pieces, pp. 28-29; Paradise, *op. cit.* pp. 56-57. The original is reproduced in Greg, *English Literary Autographs, 1550-1650* (Oxford, 1925), Pl. XIX. Lodge ended the letter with his and his wife's "humble commendacions to your Honnor and my worthy Lady, praying god continually that he will bless and enoble you both in this life and hearafter crowne you with Eternity". Compare H.M.C., *Downshire*, Vol. II, p. 189. "We here pray for some new title or honour to fall to worthy Sir Thomas Edmondes".

80. Sisson, *op. cit.* p. 110
81. See F. P. Wilson, *M.L.R.* Vol. IX, p. 99.
82. H.M.C., *Downshire*, Vol. IV, p. 215.
83. Sisson, *op. cit.* p. 112.
84. Tenney, *op. cit.* p. 177.
85. Sisson, *op. cit.* p. 117.
86. Sisson, *op. cit.* p. 161.
87. *Ibid.* p. 160.
88. H.M.C., *Downshire*, Vol. II, p. 115.
89. *Ibid.* p. xviii.

G. I. Duthie

THE QUARTO OF SHAKESPEARE'S *HENRY V*

I

In the early stages of the history of Shakespearian textual study there were in the field two theories of the relationship between the Q and F texts of *Henry V*. Upholders of a given theory might differ from one another in this or that detail: but the theories may fairly be stated thus—(i) that Q gives us the genuine text of a play distinct from and anterior to that found in F— the Shakespearian "first sketch" theory; and (ii) that the Q version is derived from that of F, is an abridgement or is derived from an abridgement of F, and was surreptitiously obtained. As supporters of (i) we may group Pope, Johnson, Knight, Collier, Fleay; and as supporters of (ii) Upton, Capell, Steevens, Malone, Boswell, Halliwell.

In 1875, for the New Shakspere Society, reprints of the Q and F texts were issued, separately, by Brinsley Nicholson. He then proceeded to prepare a parallel text edition, but, before he could finish this, illness forced him to lay it aside. P. A. Daniel undertook to complete the parallel text edition, which was published, with an introduction by him, in 1877. In this introduction Daniel states his own view in these words:

> The opinion I have formed from a careful examination, line for line, of both texts is, that the play of 1599 (the Fo.) was shortened for stage representation; the abridgement done with little care, and printed in the Qo. edition with less: probably from an imperfect manuscript surreptitiously obtained and vamped up from notes taken during the performance, as we know was frequently done. Indeed it is quite possible that the whole of the quarto edition was obtained in this manner; and the fact that it is printed from beginning to end as verse, would seem to lend some support to this conjecture. The fact, also, that the publishers of the Qos. were Millington and Busbie, and their successor Pavier, may of itself be taken as evidence that these editions are of doubtful authenticity.
>
> (p. x)

But subsequently, in the *Transactions of the New Shakspere Society*, 1880-2, Part I, pp. 77 ff., Nicholson himself published a lecture (delivered in 1879) on the relationship between the two versions, in which he argued strenuously for the theory that the Q text is that of a Shakespearian first draft.

Since this period—the late 1870s and early 1880s—most critics have taken Daniel's view, rejecting that of Nicholson. In 1920 Hereward T. Price produced a monograph, *The Text of "Henry V"*, in which he maintained that the F text is anterior to that of Q, that the Q text was procured by shorthand in the theatre, but that the work of the note-taker was supplemented by help from a traitor-actor. In 1930, Sir Edmund Chambers declared [1] of *Henry V* that "if Q1 is read side by side with F1, it is impossible to regard it as anything but a continual perversion of the same text". He summarizes the various types of corruption found in Q, and proceeds— "This corruption is far beyond what can be attributed to errors of transcription and printing, and can only be explained by some process of reporting." But between Price and Chambers, in point of time, stands an article by Hardin Craig,[2] who sides with Nicholson against Daniel. At the end of this article Craig suggests "that the manuscript from which the Quarto was printed was a genuine manuscript of the play, illegible in places and probably torn, but not the product of shorthand reporting and not showing the unmistakable characteristics of the work of a pirate-actor, ...".[3] In his recent book, *A New Look at Shakespeare's Quartos*, published in 1961, Craig handles Q *Henry V* briefly and cautiously, stating (p. 83) that "it is at least possible that the quarto is based on an earlier version of *Henry V* than that of the folio of 1623".

It is probably true to say that the view most widely held today of the Shakespeare "bad" quartos in general is that they are, at least essentially, imperfectly reported versions of the corresponding plays as they appear in the "good" quarto or folio editions, or of stage versions of these.[4] This general theory has, however, come under attack during the last dozen years, principally in America, its foremost opponents being Hardin Craig himself (in the book just cited), William Bracy, Albert Feuillerat, and Charles Tyler Prouty.[5] Bracy and Prouty are each concerned with one particular problem of textual relationship, involving in each case one of the bad quartos; but it seems clear enough that both of these critics dislike the theory of reporting as an explanation of the bad quarto texts in general as also do Feuillerat and Craig. "I suggest", says Prouty (p. 119), "that a good many 'Bad Quartos' are original plays, not reported texts."

Those who hold that a given bad quarto text is in fact derived from the corresponding good text by reporting have to face the question of the method of reporting. The formula of shorthand reporting has often been invoked, but this I must regard as quite impossible for any of the extant Shakespearian bad quartos, for reasons which will be apparent to any reader of my book on Elizabethan Shorthand (1950). Price, as we have seen, postulates for Q *Henry V* shorthand reporting supplemented by the help of a traitor-actor. The only shorthand systems known to have been available before 1600, those of Bright and Bales, were primitive and extremely cumbersome, and could have availed little, if indeed at all, for verbatim reporting at a theatrical performance. If Price's explanation

were to be accepted in full, we should have to assign to the shorthand
writer very little and to the traitor-actor a very great deal: while, on the
other hand, a reporting actor, or more than one, may well account for
everything in Q, without our bringing shorthand in at all. It is to the
formula of memorial reconstruction by an actor or actors that I would
refer the Q text.

Various textual phenomena can, of course, be explained in more than
one way, and there are differences between Q and F *Henry V* which are
consistent with both the theory of Q as a Shakespearian first draft and the
theory of Q as a corrupt report of F. But I believe that there is some evidence strongly suggesting the latter theory and definitely militating against
the former. This evidence lies in the "anticipations" and "recollections"
with which Q abounds.

II

Let us proceed now to note a few of the Q anticipations and recollections by way of example. To exclude the likelihood of visual corruption in
Q by a scribe or compositor, I choose some of my instances from anticipations or recollections of passages quite far removed from those claimed
to be memorially contaminated. In some cases, of course, it may be
suggested that we are dealing, not with an anticipation or recollection, but
with a mere coincidence. To meet this, I select some of my examples from
passages where Q also shows some metrical defect. I should reason thus.
Why suppose that in an authentic first draft Shakespeare, having written
perfectly regular verse for some time, should suddenly lapse into prosodic
uncertainty or even clumsy irregularity? This seems less probable than
that a reporter's memory has failed: and when, in the context of such
metrical uncertainty or irregularity, we find what clearly looks like an
anticipation or recollection, the temptation is irresistible to regard the
matter as indeed one of imperfect memorial transmission. In some cases
the Q corruption is too complicated and extensive to be reasonably
explained as memorial contamination introduced by a scribe who knew
the play, allowed his eye to stray off his original, and let his memory
momentarily usurp the function of his eye. As, in the examples which
follow, I explain the textual peculiarities of Q in terms of my own theory,
I hope the reader will accept the implication that other explanations have
been borne in mind and rejected as being less probable.

The Q and F line numbers in my quotations are all taken from the *New
Shakspere Society* parallel text edition.

In Act I scene ii, at line 26, Q has "No female shall succeed in salicke
land", which corresponds to F, line 41, "No Woman shall succeed in
Salike Land:". Q repeats its version of this at line 38, where the two texts
run as follows:

Q	Establisht there this lawe. To wit,	37
	No female shall succeed in salicke land:	
	Which salicke land as I said before,	
	Is at this time in *Germany* called *Mesene:*	40

F	Establisht then this Law; to wit, No Female	52
	Should be Inheritrix in *Salike* Land:	
	Which *Salike* (as I said) 'twixt Elue and Sala,	
	Is at this day in Germanie, call'd *Meisen*.	55

When he came to Q line 26, the reporter confused in his memory F lines 41 and 52-3, producing a composite line of his own. He repeated this when he came to Q line 38, and in doing so he disturbed the metre—both 37 and 39 are defective. Q is perfectly metrical for quite a stretch before 37-9, and for quite a stretch after.

At I ii 81 ff. (Q), 138 ff. (F), the two versions run—

Q	*King*. We must not onely arme vs against the French,	81
	But lay downe our proportion for the Scot,	
	Who will make rode vpon vs with all aduantages.	
	Bi. The Marches gracious soueraigne, shalbe sufficient	
	To guardyour *England* from the pilfering borderers.	85
	King. We do not meane the coursing sneakers onely,	
	But feare the mayne entendement of the Scot,	

F	*King*. We must not onely arme t'inuade the French,	138
	But lay downe our proportions, to defend	
	Against the Scot, who will make roade vpon vs,	140
	With all aduantages.	
	Bish. Can. They of those Marches, gracious Soueraign,	
	Shall be a Wall sufficient to defend	
	Our in-land from the pilfering Borderers.	
	King. We do not meane the coursing snatchers onely,	145
	But feare the maine intendment of the Scot,	

I cannot comment with any confidence on the metre here, but I would note that the Q passage seems to include a veritable tissue of memorial corruption: a comparatively large number of apparent memorial corruptions in a comparatively short passage must surely of itself suggest reporting rather than any other explanation. In Q line 81, "against the French" is modelled on F's "Against the Scot" in line 140. But then in line 82 the reporter anticipates the pattern of F line 146, a line beginning with "But" and ending with "the Scot" (accurately given in its right place in Q). And his phrase "*for* the Scot" in line 82 is probably an anticipation of F line 308—"our proportions *for* these Warres". The word "proportion(s)" constitutes a probable memorial link between F 139, Q 82 and F 308, Q 217—even though in Q 217 the link-word is converted into "collectiō" from "collected" in F 309 (F 308-9 "proportions—collected", Q 217 "collectiō—prouided").[6] Returning to the passage under examination: in Q line 85 the substitution of "guardyour" for F's "defend Our" may be due to a recollection of F line 8, Q line 4, "guard your sacred

Throne/throne". And Q's "sneakers" in line 86 for F's "snatchers" is an anticipation of F line 172, where the Scot is said to come "sneaking" (Q omits). It may be anticipation of this later passage which is also responsible for Q's substitution of *"England"* for "in-land" in line 85—cf. "England" in F 170, Q 107; though admittedly *"England"* for "in-land" might be a simple error of the aural type.[7] If we pass to the passage about the Scot coming "sneaking", we find another memorial error:

> Q   To his vnfurnish nest the weazel Scot   108
>   Would suck her egs, playing the mouse in absence of the
>   To spoyle and hauock more then she can eat.   (cat:

> F   To her vnguarded Nest, the Weazell (Scot)   171
>   Comes sneaking, and so sucks her Princely Egges,
>   Playing the Mouse in absence of the Cat,
>   To tame and hauocke more then she can eate.

Nicholson points out [8] that in line 108 (Q), 171 (F), " 'unfurnisht' is a wrong epithet and 'unguarded' a right one, for the very reason that draws the weasel is that the nest is *furnisht* with eggs." He holds that the F reading is a revision of the Q reading, failing to notice that the latter is a recollection of F line 150, Q line 90, "his vnfurnisht Kingdome" (with "the Scot" in the same line). There is absurdity in this Q reading in line 108, and also in the Q construction "To his . . . nest . . . Would suck"; and there is irregular metre in Q line 109, which is in fact a line and a half. Why should the author of an authentic first draft be guilty of gross absurdity and metrical incompetence, together, within the same short passage? Surely gross absurdity plus metrical incompetence plus a memorial error add up to reporting.

Going on to the second Act, we may note that II iv begins very badly in Q, where the first ten lines run thus:

> *King.*   Now you Lords of *Orleance,*
> Of *Bourbon,* and of *Berry,*
> You see the King of England is not slack,
> For he is footed on this land alreadie.
>   *Dolphin.*   My gratious Lord, tis meet we all goe
> And arme vs against the foe: (foorth,   6
> And view the weak & sickly parts of *France:*
> But let vs do it with no show of feare,
> No with no more, then if we heard   9
> England were busied with a Moris dance.

These ten lines correspond to 26 completely metrical lines in F. In the Q passage the first two lines together may be held to constitute a pentameter; but lines 6 and 9 are metrically defective. And the passage contains a couple of variations from F which are surely memorial corruptions. There is nothing in the first 26 lines of the F scene to correspond verbally with Q line 4, which would seem in fact to be an anticipation of F line 149, where Exeter says "For he is footed in this Land already" (Q omits). And in line

7 Q has "weak & sickly", while in the corresponding line (23) F has "sick and feeble". Here, no doubt, Q anticipates III vi 151 (F), 135 (Q), where King Henry describes his army as a "weake and sickly" guard.

So far, my examples have been of verse passages. Let us now look at a couple of prose passages, from Act III scene vi. At lines 8 ff. Fluellen proceeds thus, in dialogue with Gower, in the Q text:

> The Duke is looke you,
> God be praised and pleased for it, no harme in the worell.
> He is maintain the bridge very gallently: there is an Ensigne 10
> There, I do not know how you call him, but by Iesus I think
> He is as valient a man as *Marke Anthonie*, he doth maintain
> the bridge most gallantly: yet he is a man of no reckoning:
> But I did see him do gallant seruice.
>   *Gouer.* How do you call him? 15
>   *Flew.* His name is ancient *Pistoll*.
>   *Gouer.* I know him not.

In line 9 Q has it that the Duke is no "harme" in the world; in F the word is "hurt". Here Q may be anticipating III vii, where F (line 101) has "harme" (and where Q—line 45—has, interestingly enough, "hurt"). Again: in the Q passage we are examining, at line 10, Fluellen says of the Duke that "He is maintain the bridge very gallently", and at lines 12-13 of the Ensign that "he doth maintain the bridge most gallantly". All that corresponds verbally with this in the F version of the speech is F lines 10-11, "(He) keepes the Bridge most valiantly"; and I take it that Q is anticipating F III vi 85-6, where the same speaker, Fluellen, says "The Duke of Exeter ha's very gallantly maintain'd the Pridge", corresponding to which Q has "There is excellent seruice at the bridge", presumably recalled from Fluellen's first speech in the scene. Suppose Q were a first sketch and F a revision: we should have to be prepared to allow that in revising Shakespeare thought it worth while to change "harme" to "hurt" in III vi and to change "hurt" to "harm" in III vii—which hardly seems likely. And we should have to be prepared to allow that he changed Fluellen's "is maintain" to "keepes" at one point in III vi and inserted "ha's maintain'd" at a later point in that scene. And anyone who has studied the Q and F prose in detail will realize that, on the revision theory, we should have to suppose that Shakespeare did this sort of thing over and over again; for frequently, in the prose, F contains phrases that also appear in Q but at different points. I doubt if it is reasonable to think of Shakespeare revising in this way, though I am quite aware that this is a matter of opinion.

But another point about the last Q passage quoted above *in extenso* is that it contains a piece of nonsense. I do not think we could comfortably attribute this ineptitude to Shakespeare even in a first draft, whereas on the other hand it may well have been brought about through memorial confusion. Of the Ensign, Fluellen says (line 11) "I do not know how you call him". Yet in a moment or so Gower asks "How do you call him?" and Fluellen gives the name (lines 15-16)! How are we to explain Fluellen's

"I do not know how you call him"? The obvious explanation of the wording is that a reporter has been influenced by Gower's speeches at lines 15 and 17 (almost the same as in F). But I believe that there is an additional reason for the reporter making Fluellen here disclaim knowledge of the Ensign's name. The reporter has confused this scene with IV vii. There, in the passage from line 22 on (F numbering), Fluellen, in both Q and F, twice declares that he has forgotten a name. The first case is the name of the river in Macedon: the other is a personal name. The King, says Fluellen (F IV vii 46 ff.),

> turn'd away the fat Knight with the great belly doublet: he was
> full of iests, and gypes, and knaueries, and mockes, I haue forgot
> his name.

And Gower supplies it. (The corresponding passage in Q differs to some extent, but is to the same effect.) I think it very likely that a reporter, trying to reconstruct III vi 11, anticipated Fluellen's forgetting of a personal name in IV vii; and, for what it is worth by way of corroboration, the F passage in IV vii reads "I haue forgot his name", and at III vi 16 Q has "His name is ancient *Pistoll*", against F's "Hee is call'd aunchient *Pistoll*". And there is another possible memorial contamination of Q III vi 8 ff. through anticipation of F IV vii. In the Q passage Fluellen refers to the Ensign as "a man of no reckoning" (line 13), whereas F has "a man of no estimation"; and at IV vii 17, with Fluellen again speaking, we have in F the phrase "all one reckonings" (Q "all one reconing"). In this speech in IV vii Fluellen strings together a list of synonyms (F "pig, or the grea(t), or the mighty, or the huge, or the magnanimous"): so also in the speech at III vi 7-9, F "my soule, and my heart, and my dutie, and my liue, and my liuing, and my vttermost power". There are thus various reasons why a reporter might well mix up III vi and IV vii in his memory, and this, I think, happened.

Another passage in Q III vi which contains memorial corruption occurs at lines 51 ff. The two texts run—

Q   for look you,
      Disciplines ought to be kept, they ought to be kept.   52
            Pist.   Die and be damned, and figa for thy friendship.
            Flew.   That is good.
            Pist.   The figge of *Spaine* within thy Iawe.   55
            Flew.   That is very well.
            Pist.   I say the fig within thy bowels and thy durty maw.
                                                Exit Pistoll.

F   for discipline ought to be vsed.   52
            Pist.   Dye, and be dam'd, and *Figo* for thy friendship.
            Flu.   It is well.
            Pist.   The Figge of Spaine.   *Exit.*   55
            Flu.   Very good.

In line 52, Q's "kept" instead of F's "vsed" anticipates IV i 66-8 (F)— "when the true and aunchient Prerogatifes and Lawes of the Warres is not kept", 28-9 (Q)—"when the auncient Prerogatiues of the warres be not kept". Then at line 55 Q adds three words to the F line, and at 57 gives a line not found in the context in F. A reporter's mind has flashed back to the altercation between Pistol and Nym in II i. The passage in Q III vi recalls both the F and the Q versions of the passage in II i, for in that earlier passage "bowels" occurs in both texts, "maw" in F only, and "jaw" in Q only:

> II i F 44 ff. The solus in thy most meruailous face, the solus in thy teeth, and in thy throate, and in thy hatefull Lungs, yea in thy Maw perdy; and which is worse, within thy nastie mouth. I do retort the solus in thy bowels,

> Q 38 ff. that solus in thy throte, / And in thy lungs, and which is worse, within / Thy mesfull mouth, I do retort that solus in thy / Bowels, and in thy Iaw, perdie:

At the end of this paper, in Appendix A, will be found a further select list of probable anticipations and recollections in Q. This type of corruption is so frequent that, in my view, it would almost be enough in itself to indicate strongly the theory of imperfect memorial transmission of Q; but the case seems overwhelming when all the other types of Q corruption are added—e.g. omissions resulting in mislineation, omissions resulting in defective sense,[9] weak paraphrase, garbling, and so on.

III

Not only does the above evidence furnish us with an argument against the first sketch theory of Q: more than that—the evidence adduced in favour of that theory does not, in my view, stand up to examination. Nicholson points out that again and again F is superior to Q, and leaps to the conclusion that F is a revision of Q. But it is also possible, clearly, that in these cases Q is a debasement of F; and indeed, though Nicholson does not notice this, some of the inferior readings which he cites in Q are anticipations and recollections, memorial corruptions. I have drawn attention to some of these in my *'Bad' Quarto of "Hamlet"*, pp. 48-50.

In his 1927 article Craig hardly, in my opinion, exceeds Nicholson in cogency. Craig concentrates on two points, neither of which seems to me very strong. His first point is that "certain themes in *Henry V* are much more elaborately presented in the Folio than in the Quarto, or appear in the Folio and not in the Quarto": either these must have been amplified, or developed, in F by revision of Q, or else "in the abridgement of the play for the stage, or in process of its piracy, these themes have been specially selected for cutting"; and, he holds, "the latter alternative is unlikely, because, as Nicholson argued, they are good—obviously better than the parts retained—and because, since they are interwoven in the text of the Folio as words, phrases, and sentences, the selection of these bits would be a most troublesome and unlikely method of abridgement". He instances some of Fluellen's speeches. "In the play as we have it in the Folio," he points out, "it is Fluellen's 'humour' to refer pedantically to the art of war." This he finds to be much more marked and extensive in F than in Q. But observe his comment on IV i 65-74: here, he says, "the Quarto has the theme of Fluellen's pedantry *clearly developed*, but the Folio much more significantly" (the italics are mine). It is perfectly possible that in a memorial reconstruction a reporter might only manage to render some of Fluellen's jargon, might only manage to reflect in an imperfect way a habit of speech more fully indicated in his original (F), might only succeed in remembering the less elaborate of Fluellen's locutions. I should not here postulate the "special selection" of the more elaborate pieces of pedantry for "cutting", but simply an inadequate reportorial memory. If Fluellen talks of ceremonies and cares and forms and sobriety and modesty, I am not surprised that a reporter remembered only ceremonies and cares, and introduced fears on his own account: and if the sobriety and the modesty are the most amusing terms in the list, I am still not surprised that a reporter should miss them out, for they are the least obviously appropriate in the context, and I have little doubt that the reporter was a man of commonplace mind, pedestrian outlook, and little literary sophistication.[10] But at any rate he has managed to give us the theme of Fluellen's pedantry "clearly developed" (in Craig's own phrase). And that the Q version of this speech is in fact a piece of memorial reconstruction seems to me to be corroborated by its containing within one phrase two distinct reminiscences of passages elsewhere in the play (one anticipation and one recollection). Whereas F has "if you would take the paines but to examine the Warres of *Pompey* the Great", Q has "if you looke into the warres of the Romanes". Here the first phrase anticipates IV vii 23, F "if you looke in the Maps of the Orld", Q "And if you looke into the mappes of the worell well". It is the same speaker—Fluellen: and perhaps, in the speech in IV i which we are examining, the words "in the vniuersall World" (F), "in the worell" (Q), constituted a memorial link between the passages in IV i and IV vii. At any rate, the anticipation we have noted is a fact: and again, when in Q Fluellen says "if you looke into the warres of the Romanes", there is a recollection of F III ii 78 "the disciplines of the Pristine Warres of the Romans" and 92 "the disciplines of the Warre, the Roman Warres". This occurs in an episode totally omitted by Q, the episode involving the English, Scottish, Welsh, and Irish captains: but, though it is not found in Q, I believe this episode was in existence when the Q memorial reconstruction was made—that the reporter had some knowledge of it—and that, at the point with which we are concerned, his reconstruction in IV i was influenced by a recollection of phrasing which it contained.

Again: Hardin Craig points to a passage where, in comparison with Q, F has not only fuller expression but also a different idea. At ɪɪ iii Q 3 ff., F 7 ff., the texts run thus:

Q   *Bar.*   Well sir *Iohn* is gone. God be with him.
           Host.   I, he is in *Arthors* bosom, if euer any were:

F   *Bard.*   Would I were with him, wheresomere hee is, eyther in Heauen, or in Hell.
         Hostesse.   Nay sure, hee's not in Hell: hee's in *Arthurs* Bosome, if euer man went to *Arthurs* Bosome:

"In one case", says Craig, "she agrees that he is in heaven, and in the other she denies vigorously that he is in hell, going on then to elaborate the thought of the beauty and innocence of Sir John's death." True, there is that difference. But still, a reporter with an imperfect memory, trying to reproduce the F version, might quite easily produce the Q version instead—a briefer and simpler version, with a different turn in the thought.

More interesting, perhaps, are those passages in Q which involve the use of the French language. Craig quotes Q v ii 52-70, which corresponds to F v ii 179-190. Here there are differences: in particular, as Craig says, in Q "in this dialogue Kate takes an active part, as she does throughout the Quarto scene; whereas the Kate of the Folio, here and throughout the scene, is more reticent and ceremonious". This is true enough; but it does not necessitate Craig's explanation, that F is a revision of Q. Those passages in the play which are in French present a problem. Craig is right in claiming that "it might be thought from the appearance of the French in the Quarto that it is a mere unintelligible jumble, but in point of fact the sense can be made out without great difficulty". A phonetic method of representing the French words is used. There are frequent errors—but some of these may be compositorial misreadings. Now it is clear from comparison that, in places, the Quarto French is not an attempt at verbatim reproduction of the Folio French. But this does not necessitate the view that the Q version is the earlier. It is perfectly possible that a reporter, knowing a certain amount of French, used this knowledge so as to treat quite freely some of the passages of F which involve French. Only a quite elementary knowledge of French need be postulated, and this is not unreasonable. And a reporter who kept fairly close to his original in some places might in other places stray quite far, verbally, from that original. Craig finds that, in the wooing scene, Katharine is "more reticent and ceremonious" in F than she is in Q: we may accept this and yet say that it may be a matter of a reporter having made her less reticent and ceremonious than she was in his original.

Craig's second point in the 1927 article is that, as he claims, "in the Quarto the realistic and comic parts seem to be written in verse, which can usually, in spite of the corruption of the text, be arranged in iambic pentameter lines and scanned; whereas in the Folio many of these passages

have been definitely turned into prose". It is in his opinion quite probable
that a scene originally written in verse should have been turned into prose,
but "it is inconceivable, or at least extremely improbable, that a scene
originally in prose should have been abridged in such a way as to be turned
into verse".

Now it is true that over and over again the material corresponding to
prose in F is in Q printed as if it were verse.[11] But two observations must
be made. First, this phenomenon does not necessarily mean that the person
responsible for the Q lineation intended the material actually to be verse.
Undoubted prose set up in verse-line lengths is found in other texts also.
In the present play we may note v ii 337-42 (F), 120-8 (Q). This passage
is undeniably prose, and is printed as prose in F; in Q it is almost word for
word the same as in F, and yet in Q it is printed as if it were verse. My
second observation against Craig's position is that it is easy enough to take
almost any passage of English prose from almost any book, and break it up
so as to make it scan like verse—provided one is willing to allow on the one
hand considerable numbers of extra unstressed syllables in a given "line",
or on the other hand the omission of numbers of metrically desirable
unstressed syllables. The resultant "verse" will probably be very awkward
indeed—for, of course, it is not verse at all. And I am myself quite sure
that the passages in rough verse-line lengths in Q *Henry V*, corresponding
to prose in F, are in fact not verse at all in Q, but prose. These observations
find support in Craig's article itself. "The fact", he says at one point,
"that the Quarto is printed as verse has perhaps little significance, and it
is not always possible to be sure we are dealing with verse and not with
prose." He does think that there are some undoubted cases: yet as his final
illustration he cites a passage (the description of the death of Falstaff)
where, as he himself declares, there is "very considerable difficulty" in
reading Q as blank verse. Even a passage that he takes as convincing seems
to me very dubious. He quotes the following passage from Q (iv i 81-87):

> Euery mans seruice is the kings:
> But euery mans soule is his owne. Therefore
> I would haue euery souldier examine himselfe,
> And wash euery moath out of his conscience:
> That in so doing, he may be the readier for death:
> Or not dying, why the time was well spent,
> Wherein such preparation was made.

He should have told the reader that the word "Therefore" which he
places at the end of the second line actually occurs in Q (spelled "Therfore")
not there but at the beginning of the third line. Now all the lines here (as
he prints them) can admittedly be made to scan as pentameters. But some
of them sound awkward to my ear. With the frequent Elizabethan five-
syllabled pronunciation of "preparation", the final line is metrically
perfect. But, for the rest, I should certainly not be prepared to say, as
Craig does, that this Q passage "is probably in as perfect blank verse as
any that can be found in that version of the play". On the contrary: in

many places Q gives us passages of verse consisting of strictly regular iambic feet, as in the above quotation (apart from the last line) it does not.

IV

That Q depends ultimately on F; that Q is full of memorial corruption—too extensive and too serious to be explained as due to mere scribal or compositorial error; and that Q cannot be a stenographic report: these propositions seem to me to be clearly sound. The condition of the Q text indicates imperfect memorial transmission. And further: the condition of the Q text suggests that it is a memorial reconstruction made by actors who had taken part in performances of F or of a stage version based on F. Price [12] singles out three characters who are notably well reported: (i) Gower—"the quality of Gower's speeches is far above anything in the Quarto"; (ii) the Governor of Harfleur—he has only one speech (III iii F 44-50, Q 12-18) which "is also reported with wonderful accuracy"; and (iii) Exeter—his speeches "are marred by many faults", he "is not nearly so well reported as Gower", but "the difficult piece of Latin and French at the end of v ii is given so accurately in the Quarto, that there must have been some good manuscript before the compositor". On the identification of the reporter(s) Chambers and Greg are rather cautious. According to Chambers,[13] "Some unevenness of demerit suggests that the reporter may have been an actor. The best-rendered scenes are those in which Exeter, Gower, and the Governor of Harfleur appear. Conceivably the 'part' of one or more of these may have been available." According to Greg,[14] "In some verse speeches the texts agree closely and it is likely that one or two actors were concerned in the reporting, though the evidence is not very clear".

I believe that the evidence does suggest that actors who had played these three parts were implicated in the memorial reconstruction— probably two actors, for the small part of the Governor could have been taken by one of the others. But I find it difficult to accept the claim that the manuscript "parts" of these actors, or authentic copies of them, were available. Consider the case of Gower. It is true that he is on the whole excellently reported in Q: but this is not invariably so—there are places where his words in Q do not agree with F sufficiently closely to make dependence on an official manuscript "part" likely. Take his very first speech in the play, III ii 51-3 (F), 23-4 (Q), where F reads—

> Captaine *Fluellen*, you must come presently to the Mynes; the Duke
> of Gloucester would speake with you.

Q has—

> Gaptain *Flewellen*, you must come strait
> To the Mines, to the Duke of *Gloster*.

Here Q looks more like a memorial paraphrase of F than a version dependent on an accurately written "part". Again, a "part" would contain not only the character's speeches but the cues. In the Quarto, the cues for Gower's speeches are often enough correct, but sometimes not. At III vi 64 ff., for example, Q reports a Gower speech very well indeed (though not without quite a few small variations and omissions); but the cue is quite wrong. The preceding speech is given by Fluellen:

> F III vi 59   Ile assure you, a vtt'red as praue words at the Pridge, as you shall see in a Summers day: but it is very well: what he ha's spoke to me, that is well I warrant you, when time is serue.

> Q III vi 61   By Iesus heeis vtter as praue words vpon the bridge As you shall desire to see in a sommers day, but its all one, What he hath sed to me, looke you, is all one.

If Gower's "part" had been available, this speech of Fluellen in Q would presumably have been made to end with the word "serue": the phrase with which is does end—"is all one"—is a memorial error, an anticipation of IV vii F 29 Q 32, where Fluellen says "(')tis all one" in both texts. It may be noted in passing that the Fluellen speech in III vi contains another memorial error as well: the Q "you shall desire to see" (F "you shall see") points back a few lines to F III vi 50, "I would desire the Duke to vse . . ." (Q "I would wish the Duke To do . . .").

At certain points, then, there is evidence against the use of Gower's manuscript "part", and the high quality of the reporting of most of his speeches is rather to be attributed to the actor himself having participated in the memorial reconstruction, he not being in possession of his "part" but remembering his lines on the whole very well. As to the Governor of Harfleur: here also I cannot postulate the use of the "part", for in Q his single short speech (only seven lines) contains two verbal departures from F—"Returnes vs word" for F's "Returnes vs, that", and "dread" for "great".[15] Had the "part" been available, accurate reproduction of it would surely not have been difficult.

I have quoted Price as saying that Exeter's speeches in Q "are marred by many faults". I agree that, for the speech containing "the difficult piece of Latin and French at the end of v ii" (F lines 337-42, Q lines 120-8), a piece of authentic manuscript may have been available to the reconstructors: but we cannot suppose that Exeter's "part" was available —precisely because of the "many faults" Price refers to. Yet, despite these faults, Exeter is in the main rather well reported. Observe, for example, the condition of Q II iv. The scene falls into two portions—the section before, and the section after, the entry of Exeter. Alike quantitatively and qualitatively, the reporting is very inferior before his entry; but, as soon as he comes on, the standard improves remarkably. I have long been of the opinion that an actor who had played Exeter was implicated in the work of memorial reconstruction. He may have been in possession of the scrap of manuscript referred to above, but, except for that, he had to rely on his memory alone. I believe that any objections to the theory of his involvement can be met. Consider, for example, the opening of II ii. The first line is reported a little loosely in Q, and is unmetrical. The second line is absolutely accurate—and is spoken by Exeter. The next speech in Q is by no means perfect, but it is well reported on the whole: it is attributed to Gloucester—but in F it is spoken by Exeter. The reporter has remembered his own lines rather well: but why, it may be asked, should he assign some of them to another character? More than one explanation is possible. Remembering F line 2 and nothing between that and F lines 8 ff., and realizing that these could not very well form a single speech, he may simply have attributed lines 8 ff. to someone else, knowing that they were really his own. Alternatively (since it may be held unlikely that he would remember absolutely nothing of the dialogue between his own speeches) he may have originally reported more than Q contains: the original report may have been shortened; and, as a result of this shortening, F lines 8 ff. may have been re-assigned in Q. Again: one would expect a reporting actor to know what other characters entered along with him. In F, Exeter enters at the beginning of II ii along with Bedford and Westmoreland, in Q with Gloucester. Yet this may well reflect, not inaccurate reporting, but rather a rearrangement made in the course of an abridgement. Of course, the various lords, English and French, in the play are quite numerous, and reporters might well be forgiven for mixing them up from time to time.

V

I pass now to a consideration, in some detail, of Q as an abridgement. Chambers [16] states that "cutting may be estimated to have reduced the 3,381 lines of the play by about 1,000, making a performance in two instead of three hours possible. Eleven speaking parts are saved by the process, and this may point to a provincial performance. Some good Shakespearian matter goes, but it is of poetic rather than dramatic value." And Greg [17] states of Q that "it is certainly an abridgement, in which, for example, the whole of I i and many later passages are suppressed, but whether it is a report purposely shortened for provincial acting, or a report of such a shortened version, is not immediately apparent". He regards the former, however, as "on general grounds the more likely hypothesis". It is perfectly possible that what the reporters were trying to reconstruct was not F but an abridgement of F: but, whether that was so or not, there is evidence which suggests that, after the memorial reconstruction had been made, it was itself abridged. The strongest evidence for this relates to the total absence from Q of Act I scene i. And again I make use of anticipations and recollections. It seems clear to me that, in reconstructing I ii, the reporters (or the particular reporter concerned) were at certain points influenced by recollections of I i.

At 1 ii 3 Q has the line

> Of some serious matters touching vs and *France*.

This corresponds to F—

> of some things of weight
> That taske our thoughts, concerning vs and France.

At 1 ii 60 Q has the line

> Then amply to imbace their crooked causes,

which corresponds to F—

> Then amply to imbarre their crooked Titles,.

The Q readings "touching" for "concerning" and "causes" for "Titles" may well be derived memorially from a single short passage in F, viz. 1 i 81-3:

> And in regard of Causes now in hand,
> Which I haue open'd to his Grace at large,
> As touching France, . . .

Recollection of this at Q 1 ii 3 may be mingled with anticipation of F ɪɪ iv 152, where we have the phrase "matters of this consequence".

Let us now consider a fairly extended passage in Q—1 ii 164 ff. Considerations of space prevent my setting out the F version as well: I shall simply refer to, and quote from, the particular F lines that concern us. The Q passage runs as follows:

> *King.*   We are no tyrant, but a Christian King,   164
> To whom our spirit is as subject,
> As are our wretches fettered in our prisons.
> Therefore freely and with vncurbed boldnesse
> Tell vs the Dolphins minde.   168
>   *Ambas.*   Then this in fine the Dolphin saith,
> Whereas you clayme certaine Townes in *France*,
> From your predecessor king *Edward* the third,
> This he returnes.   172
> He saith, theres nought in *France* that can be with a nimble
> Galliard wonne: you cannot reuel into Dukedomes there:
> Therefore he sendeth meeter for your study,
> This tunne of treasure: and in lieu of this,   176
> Desires to let the Dukedomes that you craue
> Heare no more from you: This the Dolphin saith.
>   *King.*   What treasure Vncle?
>   *Exe.*   Tennis balles my Liege.
>   *King.*   We are glad the Dolphin is so pleasant with vs,
> Your message and his present we accept: 182

Corresponding to line 165 F has "Vnto whose grace our passion is as subiect" (line 244). The Q line is metrically defective: strictly speaking, it does not make very good sense—at any rate the sense is much inferior to that of F: and, in the word "spirit", it contains an anticipation of F line 257—"He therefore sends you meeter for your spirit". This F line corresponds to Q line 175: but Q line 175 has "study" instead of "spirit". Here again the sense is inferior in Q—a gift of tennis balls is suitable for a person of Henry's (alleged) temperament or spirit, but one wonders about the appropriateness of his being invited to study the tennis balls! The Q "study" is in all probability a recollection of F 1 i 44 and/or 59. This recollection occurs in Q 1 ii 175, and, two lines later, Q has "craue", the F reading being "claime". Yet again the sense is inferior in Q, for Henry is not craving the dukedoms, he is not being abject, nor does the French Ambassador think he is. It may at first sight seem foolhardy to regard this Q "craue" as originating in a recollection of "Crau'd" in F 1 i 96: but there are no less than three verbal links between the relevant contexts in 1 i and 1 ii, so that memorial confusion between the two is a definite possibility. We may set out the readings in a table:

1 i		1 ii	
F 91 Dukedomes	Q 177 Dukedomes	F 259 dukedomes	
93 *Edward*	171 *Edward*	251 *Edward*	
96 Crau'd	177 craue	259 claime	
97 hearing	178 Heare	260 Heare	

This borrowing of the verb "crave" from F 1 i comes only two lines after the Q borrowing of the word "study", also from F 1 i. And just a little later, in Q 1 ii 182, we have the reading "we accept", the corresponding phrase in F being "we thanke you for"; and at 1 i 87 F has the word "acceptance", only four lines earlier than the first of the readings from F 1 i in the above table. "Accept", it should be noted, is not the only memorial transference in Q 1 ii 182. In that line Q has "Your message and his present", whereas the F reading is "His Present, and your paines": here Q's "message" is no doubt an anticipation of that word in 1 ii 302 (F), 215 (Q). The fact would seem to be that in 1 ii 164-82 Q presents us with a whole tissue of memorial corruption, and that a significant amount of it comes from recollections of 1 i.

The reporter's, or reporters', memory of 1 i persists as late as 11 iv. At 11 iv 16 ff. Q runs—

> Question your grace the late Embassador,
> With what regard he heard his Embassage, 17
> How well supplied with aged Counsellours,
> And how his resolution andswered him,
> You then would say that *Harry* was not wilde. 20
>   *King.*   Well thinke we *Harry* strong:
> And strongly arme vs to preuent the foe.

There are some differences between this and the corresponding passage in F. Here I would only note, in particular, Q line 17 "regard" (F "great State"), line 22 "preuent" (F "meet"), and line 20, containing the word "wilde",—a line not actually paralleled in F. Here, then, peculiar to Q, we have the words "regard", "wilde", and "preuent" occurring within the space of six lines. Now in F, in 1 i, these words, or related forms, all occur

9

within five lines—F 1 i 22 "preuention", 23 "regard", 27 "wildnesse". If this is a mere coincidence, it is surely a quite remarkable one.

It would seem, then, that 1 i was in existence when the Q memorial reconstruction was being made,[18] and that the reconstructors had some knowledge of it. Why, in that case, is it altogether omitted from Q? There are other places where, with but fragmentary knowledge of an episode, the reporters nevertheless attempt some sort of reconstruction. Why not here? I believe that, in the original version of the report, an attempt was in fact made to reconstruct 1 i, and I believe that, after the original report had been made, this scene was cut out. It was removed, I imagine, as part of an abridgement process designed not only to shorten the play but also to reduce the number of speaking parts. In this abridgement, the Bishop of Ely is removed as a speaking character; for not only is 1 i absent from Q, but so also are Ely's speeches in 1 ii—all except one, but that one is assigned, not to Ely, but to an unnamed "*Lord.*". Wishing to cut out Ely, but wishing to retain this speech (1 ii F 168 ff., Q 104 ff.), the person responsible may simply have made the change to "*Lord.*" for the time being, intending that it should be decided later which lord was to deliver it.[19]

I am fairly confident, as I say, that this piece of abridgement was effected after the memorial reconstruction had been made. Could it, alternatively, be suggested that the reporters were reconstructing an abridgement in which Ely had been removed, that they had some know-ledge of the full version also, and that they allowed the latter to influence them verbally at certain points in their reconstruction of the abridgement? Important in this connection is the first stage direction in Q. Here, at the head of 1 ii, Q directs the entry of "*King* Henry, Exeter, 2. *Bishops*, Clarence, and other Attendants". Why two Bishops, when only one appears? My theory is that, in the original report, the entry of the two Bishops was correct: after the report had been made, Ely was removed; but in the reporters' manuscript, though excision of all the relevant dialogue was indicated, and though the speech-heading of Ely's one surviving speech was altered, the original stage direction at the beginning of 1 ii was, through an oversight, left unchanged. This seems to me the likeliest explanation of the facts.[20]

There are indications that other episodes which are totally omitted from Q were in existence when the original reconstruction was made. Thus, at IV vi 26-7 F has—

> with blood he seal'd
> A Testament of Noble-ending-loue:

Corresponding to this, Q has (25-6)—

> With blood he sealed. An argument
> Of neuer ending loue.

Q's "argument" is wrong here, and F's "Testament" right: for, with the former, "sealed" is pointless. The figure is of the sealing of a legal docu-ment. Now, by the F "Testament", anyone who knows the play well will be reminded of the word "attest" [21] in F III i 23; and in III i 22 F has the

word "argument". The context in F III i has various verbal links with that
in IV vi:

III i		IV vi
F 18 Noblish (misprint of Noble)	Q 26 neuer	F 27 Noble-
19 blood	25 blood	26 blood
22 argument	25 argument	27 Testament
23 Mothers	29 mother	31 mother
23 attest		

The passage in IV vi could have been memorially confused with that in III
i; I think it was, and that "argument" in Q IV vi 25 is derived from F III i
22. III i does not appear in Q at all. I should guess that, like I i, it was
deleted after the reporting had been done; but it must be admitted that
there is no definite indication of this apart from the fact that the reporters
had some knowledge of it.

There is a hint of a similar position regarding F III ii 62-136, the
episode of the English, Scottish, Welsh, and Irish officers, an episode
absent from Q. At IV i 30 Q makes Fluellen speak of "the warres of the
Romanes", while in F (IV i 69) he speaks of "the Warres of *Pompey* the
Great". As I have already suggested, the Q phrase is probably a recollection of F III ii 78—"the disciplines of the Pristine Warres of the Romans",
and/or 92-3—"the disciplines of the Warre, the Roman Warres". We may
also note F III ii 69-70—"the true disciplines of the Warres . . . the
Roman disciplines", which occurs just before the entry of Macmorris and
Jamy, but is within the episode of the officers of the different nationalities
(Fluellen's speech-heading changes to "*Welch.*" at F line 65). All that I can
claim to have indicated here is that the episode was probably in existence
when the Q report was originally made, and that the reporters remembered a phrase from it. But in view of the stronger evidence regarding I i,
it is not unreasonable to guess that this episode also was originally
reported and subsequently deleted,[22] with the saving of two speaking
parts. In Q the scene ends without an exeunt direction. It is tempting to
think of such a direction having been deleted, through oversight, at the
end of the passage of dialogue that was cut. But this cannot be pressed, for
the reporters might simply have omitted a necessary stage direction
through mere negligence.

The condition of Q in the final scene of the play provides some corroboration of the theory that abridgement was carried out in the reporters'
manuscript itself. This is a long scene in F (374 lines), and in Q it has only
142 lines. Q gives us only isolated fragments of F. Much of the wording
of Q is to be found embedded in the full text of F, but often Q uses the
phrases in a different order. Now there is one peculiarity of Q in this scene
which is very interesting. In the wooing episode, in prose, the Q lines are
frequently very short, and these are interspersed with longer ones,
occasionally much longer. Feuillerat offers an explanation of this state of
affairs. "Here", he says, [23] "the author wrote his revisions in the uneven

9*

space on the right of the page, where a scene originally in verse had been deleted. The short prose lines thus faced the longer verse, the long lines faced the shorter verse"; and the very long lines were written in the space between two lines of the deleted original. I cannot agree that we are dealing with an author's revision of an authentic original, but I believe that, with modification, Feuillerat's explanation is correct. The Q text of this episode is not that of the original reconstruction. The original reconstruction was probably much longer, and it was decided to shorten it. The person responsible simply stroked out the original report and substituted, in the margin of the reporters' own manuscript, a much briefer version (also memorial) consisting largely of scraps and phrases of the full version pieced together, often in wrong sequence. I do not think it need be assumed that the deleted original report of the episode was in verse: if the original reporters wrote their prose in approximate verse-length lines, such as we find elsewhere in Q, then conditions in the right-hand margin of the manuscript would be similar to those postulated by Feuillerat. It is not necessary, of course, to suppose that the abridgement of the original report of v ii was confined to the wooing episode. Before that episode F has 99 lines, Q only 22—and in F Exeter is present. If an actor who had played Exeter was indeed one of the memorial reconstructors, we should expect him to do much better than this. But it may be that his work here has been abridged by the simple excision of some passages.

There are considerations which suggest that in the reconstruction Erpingham may have been originally included and then removed. These considerations are rather complicated, and in dealing with them I must allow myself a good deal of conjecture. So I relegate this matter to an appendix (Appendix B), and proceed to my conclusion.

For the omission of a given passage from Q we have to consider at least three possibilities: (*a*) what the reporters were reconstructing may itself have been an abridgement of the F text, and the passage in question may have been cut in that abridgement; or (*b*) the passage in question may have been omitted by the reporters through defective memory, or perhaps for some other reason; or (*c*) the passage in question may have been cut after the memorial reconstruction had been made. I cannot point to any Q omission which gives positive evidence of (*a*), though some may indeed be attributable to it. For some, explanation (*b*) seems clearly enough to be called for—e.g. in the passage referred to in note 9 below. I have argued that in some cases (*c*) is probable, in one case extremely probable. In many cases, of course, we cannot be sure which of the possible causes actually operated. But, concentrating finally on (*c*), I would make this claim: the fact that the memorial reconstruction was probably made by actors, and that their manuscript was probably abridged after they had originally written it out, points to the theory that the motive for the reconstruction was to produce a prompt-book for provincial performances of the play. It may be supposed that the two actors in question left the Chamberlain's company, and, joining with others, proceeded to play in the provinces. They botched up a version of *Henry V* for this group. Their manuscript, after its abridgement, could not itself have functioned effectively as a prompt-book: it would hardly do to have a prompt-book indicating two Bishops when there was only one—indicating a speech as being delivered by some anonymous "Lord"—lacking necessary stage directions on occasion—and so on. Presumably the reporters' manuscript, after being shortened, was copied, and the copy (properly edited) formed the prompt-book. Later, the group sold the abridged report to be printed and published; and what they sold was not their prompt-book, but the original manuscript of the reporters in its abridged state.

APPENDIX A

I give here a list of probable anticipations and recollections in Q which are not mentioned in the body of this paper. The list makes no claim to be complete. A study of the paper and of this Appendix will indicate my belief that a reporter may anticipate a Folio reading, and then, when he comes to the later passage, he may omit or alter the reading he has already anticipated. The human memory is, of course, a complicated mechanism. The reasons for memorial association between two passages may in one case be quite clear and in another case not evident at all. Two passages may be memorially associated because of verbal links, and some of these links may disappear in Q. And so on: the subject is a complex one.

i ii Q 22 liues, your faith and seruices F 36 selues, your liues, and seruices Cf. II ii F 5 Crowned with faith, and constant loyalty Q om. | i ii Q 30 writers F 45 Authors Cf. i ii F 66 Writers Q om. | i ii Q 69 graue F 105 Tombe Cf. i ii F 233 graue Q om. | i ii Q 120 awe F 190 a rule in Nature Cf. i ii F 226 Awe Q 152 awe | i ii Q 129 behold F 199 surueyes Cf. i ii F 111 Q 75 behold | i ii Q 136 flye F 210 Come Cf. i ii F 288 Q 203 flye | i ii Q 151-2 ayde—bring F 224-6 helpe—bend Cf. i ii F 134-7 ayde—Bring Q om. | i ii Q 154 Chronicles F 232 History Cf. i ii F 165 Chronicle Q 101 Chronicles | i ii Q 170 Townes F 250 Dukedomes Cf. i ii F 154 Townes Q om., and F 210 Q 137 towne | II i Q 24 Base slaue F 28 Base Tyke Cf. II i F 89 Base is the Slaue Q 73 Base is the slaue | II i Q 72 I shal haue my F 87 You'l pay me the Cf. II i F 104 Q 86 I shall haue my | II i Q 90 troubled F 108 shak'd Cf. II iii F 20 no neede to trouble himselfe with any such thoughts yet Q 15 no such need | II ii Q 12 in the field of *France* F 16 through the force of France Cf. i ii F 131 in the fields of France Q om. | II ii Q 81 proceed F 101 extract (different construction) Cf. II ii F 53 Q 37 proceeding | II ii Q 82 truth doth showe F 103 truth of it stands off Cf. i ii F 74 some shewes of truth Q 48 some showe of truth | II ii Q 98-104 and fixed —creatures F 168-78 om.—wretches Cf. i ii F 188-90 fixed—Creatures Q 119-20 added—creatures | II iii Q 3 *Iohn* is gone F om. Cf. II iii F 17 Sir *Iohn* Q 12 sir *Iohn* and F 41 the fuell is gone Q om. | II iv Q 4 (F om.) is

verbally the same as F 149 (Q om.) except for Q on F in | ɪɪ iv Q 79 for
that cause according to F 136 To that end, as matching to Cf. ɪɪ ii F 32-5
cause—According to the weight Q 17-20 cause—According to their
cause | ɪɪ iv Q 87 you shall finde F 144 you shall reade Cf. ɪɪ iv F 38 you
shall find Q om. | ɪɪɪ v Q 6 if they passe F 11 if they march along Cf. ɪɪɪ vi
F 156 Q 138 If we may passe | ɪɪɪ vi Q 80 but when time shall serue F 80 if
I finde a hole in his Coat Cf. ɪɪɪ vi F 62 when time is serue Q om. | ɪɪɪ vi
Q 81 I shall tell him a litle of my desires F 80-1 I will tell him my minde
Cf. v i F 12-13 I will tell him a little piece of my desires Q 11-12 *I* shall
tell him, A litle of my desires | ɪv i Q 3 art thou Gentleman F 38 art thou
Officer Cf. ɪv iv F 4 Art thou a Gentleman Q om. | ɪv iii Q 57 charge F 79
places Cf. ɪv iii F 6 Charge Q om. | ɪv iii Q 59-60 to know . . . What wilt
thou giue for raunsome? F 80-1 to know . . . If for thy Ransome thou
wilt now compound, Cf. ɪɪɪ v F 64 To know what willing Ransome he will
giue Q 20 To know what willing raunsome he will giue | ɪv iii Q 92 bones
F 126 ioynts Cf. ɪv vii F 67 Q 62 bones | ɪv iii Q 95 *I* shall deliuer so F 129
I shall, King *Harry* Cf. ɪɪɪ vi F 163 Q 144 I shall deliuer so | ɪv vii Q 2 as
can be desired F 3 as can bee offert Cf. ɪv viii F 22 Q 12 (A)s you shall
desire | ɪv vii Q 60 not one aliue F 62 not a man of them that we shall take
Cf. ɪv vii F 5 Q 4 not a (B)oy left aliue | ɪv vii Q 89 To his graces will and
pleasure F 109 as long as it pleases his Grace Cf. ɪv viii F 2 Gods will, and
his pleasure Q 1 in the name of Iesu | ɪv vii Q 94 the number of the
scattred French F 118 the numbers dead On both our parts Cf. ɪv vi F 37
The French haue re-enforc'd their scatter'd men Q om. | ɪv vii Q 111
Vnder what Captain seruest thou? F 147 Who seru'st thou vnder?
(spoken to Williams) Cf. ɪv i F 93 Vnder what Captaine serue you?
(spoken by Williams) Q om. | ɪv viii Q 37 impute it to F 55 take it for
(spoken by Williams) Cf. ɪv i F 145 imputation (spoken to Williams) Q
om. | v i Q 10 discentions F 10 contention Cf. ɪv viii F 66 dissentions Q 48
dissentiõs | v i Q 38 shilling F 56 groat (to Pistol) Cf. ɪɪ i F 87 Q 72 eight
shillings (to Pistol) | v ii Q 129 Nor this haue we so nicely stood vpon F
343 Nor this I haue not Brother so deny'd Cf. v ii F 95 When Articles too
nicely vrg'd, be stood on Q om.

APPENDIX B

In F, at ɪv i 283, there is a stage direction "*Enter Erpingham.*", followed by
a five-line dialogue between him and the King, after which Erpingham
has an "*Exit.*", and the King proceeds to his soliloquy "O God of Battailes".
Now in Q, at the point corresponding to F's "*Enter Erpingham.*", we have
the direction "*Enter the King, Gloster, Epingam, and Attendants.*", this being
immediately followed by the King's soliloquy "O God of battels".
Erpingham says nothing, nor is he spoken to; and in Q there is in fact no

reason for him to be brought on at all. Different explanations of his appearance in the stage direction might be proposed: (1) the reporters may have remembered that he entered at this point, but may simply have forgotten the piece of dialogue in which he is concerned; or (2) they may have reported this piece of dialogue, and it may subsequently have been cut, but the deletion of Erpingham from the stage direction may have been overlooked.

But this Q stage direction presents a further peculiarity: not only Erpingham, but the entire direction, is unnecessary. As Q stands, when this direction occurs the King is already on the stage. The direction is also at fault in bringing Gloucester on here: he does not come on, for, after the soliloquy "O God of battels", Q has "*Enter Gloster.*", which is obviously correct. As for the Attendants: it is more proper that Henry should be alone while speaking the soliloquy (which is a prayer), than that a group of Attendants should be standing round. At the very least, they are quite unnecessary.

The whole direction is inappropriate here. But there is a point elsewhere in Q where it would have been appropriate, and it may be that, in Q as we have it, the direction has simply been accidentally misplaced.

The Q version of IV i is much shorter than that of F. The F version begins with a passage (lines 1-35) involving, as speakers, the King, Gloucester, and Erpingham (and Attendants would be in order [24]). This passage is omitted from Q. But suppose it had appeared in the reporters' original reconstruction: in that case, the Q stage direction we are examining would have been correct at the head of the scene. In F Erpingham does not enter until line 12; but the reporters might easily have brought him on at the beginning of the scene. It would be entirely consistent with the theory of Q upheld in this paper to suppose that the reporters did originally give some account of this initial passage in IV i, and that it was subsequently excised in order to get rid of Erpingham as a speaking character. If so, we must presumably take it that, after this excision had been made, the direction heading the next episode (which is reported in Q as we have it) was altered, with "*Enter the King disguised, to him* Pistoll." substituted for—perhaps—a simple "*Enter* Pistoll.". But the original direction at the head of the scene was apparently, through carelessness, not deleted.

Now by what means did this accidentally undeleted stage direction find its way into Q later on in the scene, at an unsuitable point? I am suggesting that it did: I do not know how it did; and all I claim to be able to do is to show how it could have done.

Suppose that, in the original reconstruction, IV i began at the top of a manuscript page, a page which contained material corresponding to F IV i 1-35. This we may for convenience call page (a). The abridger's pen indicated excision of the whole of this page of text, but the initial stage direction was left undeleted. The abridger then expanded the direction (?"*Enter* Pistoll.") at the top of the next page. After this, the abridger made further cancellations: most notably, he cancelled a reported version of the King's long speech at F iv i 228-83. The passage corresponding to F iv i 284-8 (involving Erpingham), if it did figure in the original report, may have occurred at the foot of a manuscript page, and may have been (intentionally) deleted along with the immediately preceding material on that page—a page we may refer to as page (x). Then page (y) began with the prayer "O God of battels", with no entry direction above it. But it may conceivably be that, through accident, page (a) was slipped in between page (x) and page (y). Thus the Q compositor would be faced with this sequence: Q iv i 114, corresponding to F iv i 227,—". . . a clipper./*Exit the souldiers*.": next, (say) two totally deleted pages,[25] the second being page (x): next, page (a), containing deleted material but also, undeleted, the direction "*Enter the King, Gloster, Epingam, and Attendants.*", which he duly set up: next, page (y), beginning "O God of battels". Gloucester's proper entry, after this soliloquy, stood properly placed in the reporters' manuscript, and appears properly placed in Q. In this way we could account for the state of affairs in Q—a state of affairs which could no doubt be equally well accounted for by modifications of this explanation, or even by other explanations. All that I am anxious to maintain here is the possibility (putting it no higher) that Erpingham appeared in the original reconstruction as a speaking character, and was subsequently cut out, just as the Bishop of Ely, and others, were cut out.

NOTES

1. *William Shakespeare*, Vol. I, p. 391.
2. *Philological Quarterly*, Vol. VI (1927), pp. 225-34.
3. The sentence quoted ends ". . . not showing the unmistakable characteristics of the work of a pirate-actor, as outlined by Messrs. Pollard and Wilson". The reference is to a series of articles on the Shakespeare bad quartos in the *Times Literary Supplement*, 1919; the article on *Henry V* is in the issue of 13 March. The theory of the genesis of the bad quarto texts propounded in these articles was abandoned by Dover Wilson long ago, and need not be examined here. But Dover Wilson still believes that Q *Henry V* is a reported version, probably "supplied by traitor-actors"—see the New Cambridge edition of the play (1947), p. 112.
4. In his *Stolne and Surreptitious Copies* (1942), Alfred Hart argues that each of the Shakespeare bad quarto versions is a derivative of the play as found in the corresponding good quarto and folio editions; and, more particularly, he holds (see p. 437) that each of the bad quarto texts "is a garbled abridgment of an acting version made officially by the play adapter of the company from Shakespeare's manuscript".
5. See Bracy, *The Merry Wives of Windsor: The History and Transmission of Shakespeare's Text* (1952), Feuillerat, *The Composition of Shakespeare's Plays* (1953), and Prouty, *"The Contention" and Shakespeare's "2 Henry VI": A Comparative Study* (1954).
6. See the remarks at the head of Appendix A in this paper.

7. Errors due to mishearing, or to misunderstanding of what had been heard, are consistent with various methods of transmission by reporting, but by themselves they do not, of course, indicate such transmission. Examples of probable or possible errors of hearing in Q *Henry V* are—I ii 45 "the function" for "defunction", I ii 76 "Foraging" for "Forage in", III vi 87 "partition" for "perdition", III vi 99 "abraided" for "upbraided", III vi 132 "heire" for "air", III vii 44 "his" for "is", IV iii 82 "flouendry" for "slovenry", and IV v 12 "Why least" for "Whil(e)st".

8. *Transactions of the New Shakspere Society*, 1880-2, Part I, p. 85.

9. E.g. in Canterbury's long speech at I ii F 35 ff., Q 21 ff., the Q version on occasion parallels that of F in phrases which, on account of omissions in Q, become nonsensical—Q 47 has "*Hugh Capet* also", as has F 71, but because Q omits to mention King Pepin (F 67) its "also" is absurd; and Q 51 speaks of "*Charles*, the foresaid Duke of *Lorain*", as does F 85, but because Q omits F 72 its "foresaid" is absurd. See Daniel's introduction to the parallel text edition, pp. xi-xii. This genealogical speech in Q is in part incoherent, so that its omissions would seem to be not a result of deliberate abridgement, but rather a result of defective memorial transmission. A scribe or compositor would not, one presumes, have made such a botch of it. It is true that one of the Q omissions, F 77-84, may be a compositorial error—the eye could have jumped from "*Lingare*" at the end of F 76 to *Ermengare* (with similar termination) at the end of F 84: but this may not be the explanation (if both names stood in the "copy" for Q, they need not have had the same termination), and in any case this particular omission is not relevant to the absurdities I have mentioned.

10. As will later appear, I believe there were two reporters. When I speak of "the reporter", I mean the reporter responsible for whatever passage is under discussion. My impression that neither of the reporters had very extensive literary talents is based on the state of the Q text as a whole.

11. "As a paradoxical result," says Chambers, "Pistol's speeches resume verse form" (*William Shakespeare*, Vol. I, p. 391).

12. *The Text of "Henry V"*, p. 19.

13. *William Shakespeare*, Vol. I, p. 391.

14. *The Shakespeare First Folio* (1955), p. 283.

15. It is possible that these two Q readings are memorial errors. "Returnes vs word" may contain an anticipation of F III v 69, "And quickly bring vs word of Englands fall" (Q omits). And "dread King" may contain a recollection of I ii F 99 Q 63, "dread (S)oueraigne", F 105 Q 69, "dread Lord". I claim no more than that this is possible.

16. *William Shakespeare*, Vol. I, p. 392.

17. *The Shakespeare First Folio*, p. 282.

18. All that has been proved, of course, is that Q at certain points echoes wording which is found in F I i. Logically, it does not follow that, when the memorial reconstruction was made, I i existed in exactly the same form as is found in F. But common sense suggests that this is a reasonable assumption.

19. In the introduction to the parallel text edition, Daniel notes (p. xii) that there are certain historical errors in F which are not found in Q, and he holds that it is a case of these errors having been deliberately corrected. F gives I ii 168 ff. to Ely, but the Chronicles assign it to Westmoreland. When in the Q version it was given to "*Lord.*", it was intended, according to Daniel, "to lump it with Exeter's following speech; Westmoreland's part being cut out". Chambers (op. cit. p. 392) declares that "the historical corrections attributed to Q by Daniel are . . . illusory". Greg (op. cit. p. 283) does not seem quite so confident as Chambers about this.

Even if Daniel is right, my main contention remains unaffected, viz. that in Q Ely as a speaking character is completely cut.

20. The theory has been suggested, and also opposed, that the material available as "copy" for Q included a "plot": see Barbara Damon Simison in *Philological Quarterly*, Vol. XI (1932), pp. 39-56, and a rejoinder by Price in the same periodical, Vol. XII (1933), pp. 24-32. Chambers (op. cit. p. 391) says that a "plot" was conceivably available, "since a few marginal notes for action are common to Q1 and F. But if so," he adds, "it was a very skeleton one." Greg (op. cit. p. 283) states that "three notes of action appear in both texts at the same point, but such action is implicit in the text and no reference to a 'plot' need be assumed". It might be suggested, I suppose, that the two Bishops in our stage direction came from the "plot" of the full version of the play, while the Q text is a report of an abridgement: but there is in fact no clear evidence of a "plot" behind Q, and the line of argument I have taken seems to me more likely.

One can hardly leave the initial stage direction of i ii without noting another oddity. F includes Clarence among the nobles who enter, though he (with others) is mute. Q also gives Clarence an entry, and he is likewise mute. Greg (*The Shakespeare First Folio*, p. 287) says that how Q came to know Clarence's name here is a puzzle. Clarence does not appear anywhere else in F. In Q he does appear in iv iii, and speaks. I take it that the reporters were simply confused about the various lords and on occasion just named them as they wished.

21. If "Testament/attest" was indeed a memorial link between the two passages in the mind of one of the reporters, this particular link has disappeared in Q, for neither word occurs in the context in Q iv vi. See the remarks at the head of Appendix A.

22. Greg (*The Shakespeare First Folio*, p. 282) suggests that this episode "must surely have been cut when the play was acted before James I in 1605". We may admit this: but was it censored earlier? Greg thinks it may have been. Chambers (*The Elizabethan Stage*, Vol. I, p. 323, note 2) quotes from a letter written to Burghley from Edinburgh, dated 15 April 1598: "It is regretted that the comedians of London should scorn the king and the people of this land in their play; and it is wished that the matter should be speedily amended lest the king and the country be stirred to anger." This was presumably written before Shakespeare had even composed the episode in question. It does not follow from the Scottish letter that the episode was suppressed in the London performances prior to 1600 which the reporters were remembering. The protest may not have been effective, or not effective in all cases.

23. *The Composition of Shakespeare's Plays*, p. 54.

24. F names Bedford in the opening stage direction of the scene. He is addressed, but does not speak. He may be regarded as an "attendant".

25. We may postulate two pages if, in the original report, the material corresponding to F iv i 228-88 was reconstructed fairly fully. We could postulate just one page (page (x) itself) if that material was reconstructed only sketchily.